THE HR CYNIC'S READER
by Edward Moss

Dedicated to all those, who, over the years, have themselves suffered mismanaged and intolerable HR practices

First Edition © Edward Moss 2016
Second Edition © Edward Moss 2022

ISBN: 9798831783902

THE HR CYNIC'S READER

Introduction

Having written *'The Marketing Cynics Reader'* some years ago (now available for £1 in all good bookshop bargain bins) very much based on my years of experience in marketing communications, a friend of mine suggested that given my utter loathing and contempt for HR (Human Resources), I should perhaps write an equivalent *'HR Cynics Guide'*.

So, having undertaken much research, and now free from the constraints or repercussions of reporting on those with the power to hire and fire (now just a grumpy old man no longer needing needless and often farcical interviews), I discovered that I knew as much about HR as the average HR practitioner - that is, virtually nothing (sorry, I do sincerely fully acknowledge my harshness towards those who are professional, dedicated, hard-working and honest personnel people).

My friend and I concluded that armed with this total and complete lack of knowledge about the subject, I would indeed be extremely well-placed to write an objective book about it.

Or was that an objectionable book?

Either way, my conviction is that many of the loathsome, deeply mistrustful and often quite facile practices in HR today are very much responsible for the malaise that has struck modern recruitment and employment in the UK. It now firmly seems to take one step forwards and two, if not three steps back on almost a daily basis in terms of both quality and ethics.

And it's not that HR people are necessarily bad people at all; thankfully, as should be the case, the healthy majority of them are nice, upstanding, fellow human beings. It's just so many are by and large so dreadful at what they do. And that is with all the university training and an armful of accreditations.

Or good at what they can't and don't do.

And the actual *'profession'* (maybe it's vying with the position of oldest profession in the world – they have a lot in common!) itself has become a total and expensive waste of space, time and trouble.

I'm speaking from bitter experience, in fact very bitter experience, having on one occasion having been at the receiving end of the most amateurish, dishonest and corrupt HR procedures I have ever encountered in my entire working life.

Rather sadly, I had to walk away with a *'financial result'* prior to it being heard at tribunal.

At the time, I really regretted not having sufficient funds in the bank to allow me have my day at the tribunal so I could have fully exposed the entire evil charade and the witless, dishonest and downright clueless people perpetuating it.

This was especially annoying, as I had the business editor of the local regional newspaper chomping at the bit to attend the proceedings and expose the lot of them, including their rather aggressive and quite nasty (and in the opinion of my own solicitor, almost bordering on the unethical) legal people who seems happy to represent the charade (and why not - they were being well-paid and we all know that the law can be a total ass at times, preferring money over what it morally just).

Unfortunately, as with all cowards who are frightened of having their sordid truths exposed, there is now a gagging order in place, as plainly those who construed the whole affair are extremely embarrassed that it might get out.

Certainly, I have noticed that the person at the centre of this sordid affair never put this particular travesty in their HR *'career'* on their LinkedIn (the business networking) profile.

As witnessed on the rogue trader segment of the BBC's *'Watchdog'* consumer programme, those who are the guiltiest and/or the most embarrassed always seem to seek the most anonymity.
And an interesting aside.

I read a while back that Oskar Gröning, the *'Bookeeper of Auschwitz'*, following his release from a POW camp in 1947, worked in . . . . . . yes, you guessed . . . . . the personnel department of a Hamburg factory, later becoming an honorary judge of industrial tribunal cases.

You couldn't make it up.

If the cap fits! Hmmm!

HI-HO, HI-HO, IT'S HR, OFF WE GO…..

Chapter 1

Now, personally, I hold HR somewhat responsible for at least three (if not perhaps a lot more) percentage points of any current and recurring unemployment figures. Although at the time of updating this to its second edition, thanks to pandemics and leavings of the EU, the number of available jobs outstrips the number of workers available for the first time.

According to current ONS (Office for National Statistics) statistics, vacancies across the UK in 2022 have outstripped the number of people looking for work, with the UK labour market continuing to get squeezed to the extent the pips have fallen out.

The latest data from the ONS, to March 2022, was showing that the unemployment rate was continuing a downwards spiral, decreasing by 0.1% over the previous quarter to 3.7% and to quite historic lows, in fact the lowest level since the mid-1970's.

Conversely, available jobs across the entire UK economy were continuing to rise to a record almost 1.3 million.

This saw demand in the labour market forge ahead of people supply for the first time since record keeping began. Numerous factors have contributed to this, including the self-repatriation of workers from the EU leaving jobs that some indigenous British people have a habit of thinking are below them.

I feel that if we all went back to good old-fashioned personnel managers who actually knew about the needs of the business they are employed by; who cut out all the hyperbolic time-expansion activities they are so expert at using (or abusing); who have a precise knowledge of the skillsets their workers have or need when it comes to vacancies and have some form of inkling of the function of the business they are employed by, employee candidates, employees and the business owners/bosses, would all be far better off.

And productivity throughout the land, if not the world, would be so much higher.

But no.

From an external perspective, HR people always **look** very, very busy. As busy as Sharon and Tracey used to be on a Monday behind the counter in Woolworths, (remember Woolworths?), chatting together about their weekend conquests while the customer patiently waited to be served. And then, when the customer asked for an item they couldn't find on the shelves, the reply from Sharon or Tracey would inevitably be, *'Oh, we haven't that, but we do get asked a lot for it'*.

And we all wonder why Woolworth's failed? In fairness, this was combined with their habit of demoting Ladybird, their own brand of children's clothing, to the rear of their shop, placing far more emphasis and importance on 80p a shot pic'n'mix and their display of the otherwise diminishing national, if not worldwide demand for CDs and DVDs.

However, in reality, nobody really knows what HR actually, if indeed anything, does. They tend to while away their time between pay cheques, arranging god-forsaken bonding sessions in some far-flung three-star hotel that sees grown adults jumping up and down on coloured squares in time to appalling, loud music.

Or *'bonding sessions'* as they refer to them.

However, if truth be told, Gorilla glue and two pieces of wood provides a far better bonding session.

Failing that, they organise for staff to make Origami characters or give feedback on the company that the HR person notes down in a very sincere and soon-to-be-binned manner on their HR clipboard, all this taking place in said far-flung three-star hotel.

Yes, that keeps them quite content with their lot.

The recruitment industry itself is also in dire need of official regulating, and not in an official, slap on the back self-regulating manner (that they are so good at) either.

It is just so extremely bad at, and often quite disreputable in, what it does. Although in fairness, as anyone would, these people are simply seizing a business and subsequent profit opportunity readily provided for them by those dozy and dysfunctional internal company HR people, who, instead of dazzling their chief executive and directors with brilliance, have baffled them with 100% total and complete, utter nonsense, straight out of a manual.

What is actually very sad is, that over the past 35 years, bearing in mind the number of different organisations I have worked for, and the number of friends and acquaintances I have, I can't even count on two fingers (yes, those same fingers otherwise reserved for a reverse-Churchillian greeting as the HR manager runs off to one of many life-savingly vital meetings held each day) the number of people who have ever had, or more worryingly, currently have, a good word for HR.

And while it may be said that fools seldom differ, equally, sixty million people can't be wrong. No one has a particularly good word for HR, and that's even with taking the hiring and firing aspect out of the frame.

Generally, the only fools who don't differ are the HR people. Those honourable members of the clinically useless happy-clappy club.

This surely cannot be right for a function that is allegedly a profession and something equally and allegedly core, so we are made to believe, to the running of a business. Or is it the running-down of a business.

Or even a spelling mistake and the potential 'ruining' of a business?

It must be so intrinsically malfunctioning as an industry if it can garner only two positive comments from the thousands of people from all walks of life I have known over 35 years!

And what's more worrying is, that within this huge group of detractors, are a former Government minister, a former major UK city council leader and two chief executives of very large multinational companies (the latter two who used to do the hiring and firing personally themselves, both employing excellently efficient administration seniors to carry out day-to-day personnel affairs).

However, so as not to appear a total misery and just a grumpy old man, I have to manly admit that I have actually come across quote a few extremely good, if not absolutely excellent personnel people over 35 years, three in particular who stick in my mind for being both extremely affable and 100% professional.

I will not mention names, but one worked for a major UK motor manufacturer, one as training manager at a business charity, and the other for the business school at a university. These were proper, professional, dedicated, personnel people; people you could not only have a social natter over lunch with, but ones who would lend a professional ear when needed and did their level-best to help where they could.

And most importantly, ones you could not only get good advice from, but actually trust and rely on. Which in fairness is a rather rare ability in any field of business, let alone HR.

Similarly, I once worked for an organisation where I was engaged, in the absence of the Head of HR who was on leave, by her subordinate who had joined the business two weeks previously.

Not that I am decrying anyone taking leave. And I am all for delegation by management to their subordinates, but there is the notion here of taking this all a bit too far. A bit of forward planning could so easily ensure that the person ultimately responsible for recruitment should be actively involved in the recruitment process of staff (she was simply on holiday and not on special leave, so not much sympathy from me I'm afraid). So, if she couldn't plan her interview schedule, I did wonder how she managed anything else.

While I did get to meet and speak with this particular Head of HR several times (she was, as it happens, actually a pleasant, affable lady), and she joined us for lunch a couple of times in the office complex restaurant.

Then the bit you couldn't make up happened.

She asked me over lunch on one occasion three months later *'What is it exactly you do?'*

Having sent, and had published, several press releases in the media, re-written the organisation's prospectus, arranged an interview for the CEO on the BBC and written some case studies, I was, to say the least, somewhat astounded. Not the most intellectual of questions from a *'senior executive'* earning back then, £60,000 (the equivalent of around £80,000 at the time of this second edition update).

Now, I'm not for one moment suggested that we all never cut corners if we can, or are perhaps a little lax ourselves in our own areas of business specialism.

We are, after all, human! But, so blatantly not knowing what one of your employees does in the business!

A very good friend of mine (equally as dismissive of HR as I am) is rather quick with his quotes. When he heard I was writing this (the original) book, he reminded me that if a business was to rid itself of its HR department, the response from workers would be very much like the reply from American satirist Dorothy Parker, when she was told that President Calvin Coolidge had died.

At the time, she responded, *'How can they tell?'*

Now, let's get ready to rumble!

Chapter 2

It would appear, according to the Chartered Institute for Personnel and Development (CIPD), that way back in 1913, some *'extraordinary and enlightened people'* (oh, please, do give me strength! As Jim Royle, played by English actor Ricky Tomlinson in the comedy series the Royle Family used to say, *'Enlightened my *rse!'*) came together to form what is now the *'wunnerful'* CIPD.

Well, despite being, as they claim, *'an internationally recognised brand'* and having over 160,000 members, if modern day HR practices are anything to go by, they really needn't have bothered. While the going is good, I can only suggest they need to sell their office and open a fish and chip shop instead. Far more useful. Feeding the masses real food rather than bin fodder. Sadly, I doubt they would even remember to turn the fish fryer off at night.

The group of *'extraordinary and enlightened people'* really ought to have stayed at home knitting, wondering how their grandchildren's family would cope with Sky box remote-control arguments, talking about the then threat to world peace (now as I update this book, there's something that hasn't changed much) or preparing themselves for the twitter revolution that was to start some 100 years later.

Or alternatively, and more productively, watching slow-drying paint, er, dry.

Providing, that is, they could actually stay either awake or for that matter, alive long enough.

The simple fact is that despite what the CIPD or their 160,000 paying members may say, HR has become a roller-coasting (accent on the *'coasting'*), over-valued, overpaid and totally overblown dysfunction, contributing relatively nothing more to the business than a far better value-for-money administrative assistant could do. Although, should an experienced administrative assistant seize hold and do it, they would probably do it with altogether much more forthright efficiency.

And without - as is the case with certain taxpayer-funded outfits such as a certain UK national broadcaster, who employ these professional misfits, paying ridiculous six-figure salaries - rewarding their failure with otherwise unbelievably, in the context of the commercial world, huge bonuses and golden hellos and goodbyes.

Incidentally, one particular Head of Human Resources at the BBC, Lucy Adams, was once branded as a liar by the Chair of the Public Accounts Committee (PAC), the Right Honourable (and wonderful) Margaret Hodge.

Mrs. Hodge has never been one to hide her light under a bushel when it comes to berating the useless, so the fact she did so here lends credence to the fact that HR can at times be really a total nonsense.

Although not in receipt of a golden goodbye herself (plenty of cheers from staff though - Lucy Adams oversaw £20 million of public money go towards executive pay-offs at the BBC).

She had received a staggeringly eye-watering £320,000 (also from the hard-pressed license fee-payer) a year salary for her efforts. That's a salary way in excess of twice that of the Prime Minister of the UK (£142,500 at the time of writing, now £161,401 in 2022), a man who runs the country and reports back to Her Majesty the Queen! All at the same time as BBC journalists on the firing line in the worlds' war zones had their pay frozen. Not that I'm especially crying at their own six-figure salaries (also care of the hard-pressed license fee-payer).

The usual *'going rate'* utter rubbish excuse was – as it always is - cited as the reason (lame excuse more like) for her unbelievably excessive salary by then director general Mark Thompson.

In fact, when being scrutinised by Mrs. Hodge, Ms Adams had the bear-faced cheek and utter gall to laughingly tell the PAC that she was *'seriously undervalued compared to her equivalents working for FTSE 100 companies'*. By the same twisted logic, then the Prime Minister must be criminally undervalued. But to say *'seriously undervalued'*. If nothing else, this type of egotistical self-adulation just goes to reinforce her total unsuitability.

Aside from the simple fact that one could actually ever place any sort of worth whatsoever on an HR director, let alone an undervalue, is in itself so totally music-hall farcical.

And if she was undervalued, I'd hate to think what an efficient, forthright and actually pro-active HR director would be worth!

It is interesting that Richard Ingrams, editor of *'The Oldie'* (and one-time editor of *'Private Eye'*), made the observation that seeing as HR people are always so keen for candidate CV's to contain the most up to date references, would Miss Adams be including the comments attributed to her by Margaret Hodge on her own CV, namely:

'I'm not having any more lies this afternoon; you're developing a habit of changing your evidence.'

Undoubtedly, pigs will fly first. And quite low in the atmosphere too.

Duck your head now.

The *'going rate to get the best'* excuse has got to be one of the most overused and unbelievably stupid, wicked and untruthful statements in recruitment today. It is total rubbish. Councils throughout the land certainly don't pay the *'going rate to get the best'* (perhaps not even one-twentieth of this BBC woman's annual remuneration) to engage the services of street cleaners, yet they get people who do an admirable and excellent job.

People who in the main take great pride in their jobs, taking into account they are cleaning up after thoughtless, inconsiderate and ignorant members of the public.

Bargain chain shops similarly don't pay their cashiers more than they have to (yet strangely, the owners of both Home Bargains and B&M have appeared in the middle to upper rankings of the Sunday Times Rich List - which details the minimum wealth of Britain's 250 richest people or families - for several consecutive years now) putting up with ignorant customers on their phones, people who never even utter a simple *'thank you'*.

I buy some of my basics in my local pound shop precisely because I love the wonderfully friendly ladies who check out my goods and make me feel great, never failing to put a smile on my face.

All somewhat better than an egotistical and vastly overpaid HR hatchet-merchant.

I'll be referring to that one about over self-valued *'going rate'* later, wondering how the attracted best in the banking industry, with their huge, unforgivable bonuses.

How that could have justified it all by saying such a statement based on the £500billion (that's £500,000,000,000) the UK government had to shove into curing the 2008 financial crisis caused by those salaried at the *'going rate to get the best'* who had been attracted by said *'going rate'* by the astute and wide-awake banking HR industry defies belief.

Eyes wide shut more like!

Meanwhile, HR continues to clap itself on the back at every available opportunity, providing a crutch for cowardly and useless CEO's who are beaten into submission by HR jargon. They often don't, for even one fleeting moment, realise how the morale of their workers, or for that matter, the quality of their business and its bottom line, are constantly and negatively being impacted upon by these sometimes dangerously, incompetent people.

HR has often been described as *'Human Remains'*, or the *'Business Prevention Unit'*, demonstrating exactly how well thought of HR actually is by staff. For example, how many times have you seen equivalent negative descriptions by staff for their sales, transport (sorry, I should say *'logistics'*) or payroll counterparts?

Exactly. In comparison, almost nil.

Value and worth, eh?

Now, I should once again at this juncture add that there are some good - in fact some excellent - personnel people out there. Equally, there are some good recruitment companies and consultants. But these are, sadly, in a minority.

It's become the thing to do if you are made redundant and have a few pounds to spare. Start a recruitment consultancy. It's cheaper than starting an estate agency. You don't need a high street office and you won't need to use a tape measure and a camera to upload highly flattering pictures of utter hovels. Although the principles are the same.

Make sure you fool all of the people all of the time and not just some of the people some of the time.

You don't need qualifications and you certainly don't need any common sense. Just a computer linked to the internet, a little expertise with copying and pasting, and the ability to make everything up as you go along that you otherwise can't copy and paste from existing sources of nonsense and hyperbole.

You then start **all** your recruitment advertisement with *'My client is a leading . . . . .'* despite the fact they **are not your client** (you probably only contacted them after they omitted *'no agencies'* from their most recent recruitment advertisement) and you have **no proof whatsoever** that they are actually *'leading'* anything. You just say they are leading in order to give them a big head so they will pay you for the recruitment service you are providing. One they really didn't need in the first place.

That is what the internal HR people should be doing. The recruiting. Because they are supposedly the ones who know the business and the staff and positions needed to run the business.

After all, if you have an internal design team, you don't subcontract your design work to an outside designer. Or if you run a restaurant and have a kitchen, you don't sub-contract your food preparation to the take-away next door! Although some of the discoveries by the television consumer programmes might not bear the latter out fully.

Now, before we go and dissect, cut up, play with or even, dare I suggest, discard HR like it really deserves, I'm going to start at the front and then whiz to the back.

I wrote the following fake advertisement many years ago in response to the downright dishonest recruitment advertising that was starting to spring up in the early 1990's. I even received a bottle of Champers and a box of choccies from the publication that featured it on their letters page.

I was, at the time, in the market for a new job and found frustration and despondency setting in at the unbelievably *'high'* levels of quality recruitment I witnessed daily.

Yes, I know, sarcasm is the lowest form of wit.

But according to the advertisements on the job boards, the recruitment specialists were all recruiting for *'leading'* companies, and what better a type of company to work for than a leading one. Yes, every single, last one of them, according to their recruitment consultant, was a leader, although I have been trying to find any actual proof of their *'leadership'* for many years now.

I searched high and low, without as much as a single shred of evidence produced. I even looked under the sink – but at least there I found the bag of Euros I knew I had somewhere, but hadn't been able to locate in time for a break in Spain two months previously.

So, I wrote an advertisement for the job I didn't want. It contained the exact sentiments I felt were lurking behind every single recruitment consultant's offering.

attractive salary - well, as it's so low, it's extremely attractive to us

plus benefits - tea and biscuits are free and you get to keep any un-franked stamps you steam off incoming mail

Northern-based - Inverness-ish

pleasant rural surroundings - at our head office 48 miles outside the Inverness-ish location

good local facilities - the Government haven't shut down the local Post Office or uninstalled the sole cash machine.........yet

car scheme - you go to the local garage and buy a car. We've negotiated 25% discount, but due to location, the car costs 30% more than an equivalent one bought in Lancashire, so you make a net gain of approximately minus 5%

non-contributory pension scheme - well, we certainly don't contribute to it (yes, I know, firms have to now contribute by law)

fantastic opportunity - we can't find any other shmucks idiotic enough to take the job

progressive company - we never pay you on the same day each month

one of the UK's top - there are only 3 other UK companies daft enough to be in the same business

market leader - see previous point

impressive range of clients - three *'cheap because goods are near their sell-by date'* stores in Birkenhead, Scunthorpe and Dunstable respectively, a Chinese Takeaway in the Midlands, and a ball-bearing manufacturer in Devon

knowledge of Windows useful - because our window cleaner left three weeks ago
IT literate - well we don't know how to work the blasted computers, do we? Er, Windows or Mac? Well, you can't eat a Windows, can you?
educated to degree level - we have to say this to look good, and anyway, we want some person who knows nothing about business but at least is well-educated and dirt-cheap
one of the UK's fastest growing - we keep increasing the prices of our products
some international travel - we have two foreign offices, one in Tehran, the other in northern Alaska
highly-respected organisation - bankrolled by the Mafia, so you better respect us, OK!
mustn't be a clock watcher - we expect a 10-hour day from you so our directors can enjoy their golf uninterrupted
must be a team player - we like to challenge the business next-door to 5-a-side football when business is slow
must be a self-starter - we haven't actually got a clue yet what it is we want you to do
you will manage a team of four - the tea lady, toilet attendant, security guard and the rap-obsessed Youth Trainee who can't pronounce basic English words correctly and complains about the sun in his eyes yet insists on wearing his baseball hat back to front
your contribution will be acknowledged - the MD will thank you each time you lend him a fiver when the petty cash tin is empty
OTE £45,000 - your basic is £11,000; however, you might well achieve £45,000, after 25 years' service that is. Meanwhile, your starting salary is definitely £11,000

performance-related bonus - depends on how good you are at Karaoke

generous holiday scheme - we own a two-bed chalet at Butlin's in Skegness which you can use free of charge during the Winter

previous applicants need not apply - we had only two applicants last time - one a serial mugger, the other a reformed arsonist

apply to our retained consultants - seeing as we haven't a clue ourselves

who will shortlist suitable candidates - they don't have a clue either

my client is a market leader - because they were the ones who were stupid enough to forget to put *'no agencies'* at the bottom of their advertisement in the paper. And our consultant calls all his clients leaders, even the jailed financial consultant who conned hundreds of thousands of pounds in savings from unsuspecting pensioners

a second language would be an advantage - the accountant who does the wages speaks only Portuguese

good prospects - you're bound to want to leave in a couple of years to go to a proper and better-paid job

Yes, *'leading'*, possibly the worst and most abused word in recruitment land, apart from the beloved and equally abused *'solutions'*. (HR Solutions – I presume that's Alka Seltzer, which, as a solution, is the best one to cure those stomach ills given to workers after consuming too much HR bull).

Then there's the recruitment consultants themselves.

Is there any particular reason why some recruitment consultants copy and paste direct application job advertisements from, as an example, the NHS job website, and then claim them as *'my client'*? A client they surprisingly can't actually mention, side-by-side with salary details they appear to have no idea about?

They don't even change the font of the copy and paste to match that of their email font.

In fact, they are sometimes as brazen as to ask you, the candidate, what your salary expectations are. Plainly because they don't know themselves, and the client they don't really have (the one they allegedly represent, the *'my leading client'*) won't tell them anyway.

Or, they say salary '*neg*' which presumably means either negative, negligible, neglected or negligent.

Can you imagine? A *'leading client'* with a *'multi-million pound'* turnover who doesn't see fit to state what salary they are offering? Preposterous! This is the equivalent of driving your car into a petrol station for fuel without a clue as to whether it takes petrol or diesel, and then having no money to pay for it either way!

Is this not wasting applicants' time and immorally raising their hopes?

I'm sorry, but it's the height of irresponsibility, and certainly one aspect of many in recruitment that needs addressing as a matter of urgency.

Even instituting the simplest of mini '*charters*' for applicants who respond to an agency recruitment advertisement (rather than the usual, unqualified *'we are a leading recruitment consultancy*' nonsense) might help separate the wheat from the totally useless chaff majority.

Perhaps something along the lines of:

'This is a genuine employment position and we guarantee that we are genuinely working solely/in conjunction with x corporation in filling this position.'

There should not have to be a *'buyer beware'* attitude for job seekers, especially in hard times.

It's not like hawking a customer into buying a mobile phone they want that does everything they don't need, such as Instatweet, Facetok and Comparetheripoff, but is missing a simplistic way of actually making phone calls, thereby selling people the functional phone they actually need.

This is all about employment, life, family and the future.

We've all had unsolicited phone calls from recruiters, some excellent, some a patent waste of time, but this *'my client'* nonsense, when it is in reality NOT in any way *'my client'* at all, really has to stop.

Now another aspect that needs addressing.

Some organisations have the stupid system where they have several *'preferred'* recruitment consultants working for them at one time. Common sense dictates that job candidates, especially in specific sector professions or trades, will more than likely, without exception, be registered with each of the preferred trade recruitment agencies anyway so as to have all their employment avenues open.

Not alone that, but each of the preferred agencies will no doubt use the (cheap) electronic employment bulletin boards, so the same advertisement will be repeated all over the place, sometimes just with subtle differences to try and fulfil the *'my client'* tomfoolery claim.

Again, this wastes applicants' time and unnecessarily raises their hopes, because the agencies certainly don't tell candidates that another eight recruitment consultancies are also involved in the same, identical candidate search.

Instead, what they do is ask you to sign an agreement that they are acting on your behalf. Covering their backs in case the main recruiter actually comes to you with an offer of applying for the job directly, thus cutting the consultant out of their commission.

Or for that matter, if you come across the original advertisement from the company itself, where they have omitted the *'no agencies please'* (but by then the recruitment consultant will have completely buggered up any opportunity you might have had of applying directly yourself).

Yet another very annoying habit some of the employment agencies demonstrate is recruiting for people way outside their own location. I appreciate some agencies will be on the roster as a group for multi-nationals, but when an independent recruitment consultancy based in Exeter starts canvassing in Leeds for a position in Falkirk when they have absolutely no connection with either the company or location, I'm sorry, this is just not on.

I could suggest the perhaps the CIPD might do something about this, but I'm not that naïve. I do appreciate they are an extremely busy organisation with ever so much very important work to do. There's Americanised HR rubbish to import for passing on to its 160,000 members so they in turn can organise worthless and often intimidating happy-clappy jumping-up-and-down-on-coloured-squares bonding sessions for staff. Bonding sessions designed by some witless American wah-wah, awesome, sick, epic or whatever adjective is flavour of the day, for an audience so off-target that even the equivalent proverbial hedgehog thrown at a dartboard would still miss it and hit the wall.

As I mentioned earlier, perhaps it needs intervention by DWP, or another Government department - even dare I suggest the Department for Business, Energy and Industrial Strategy (yep, yet another relatively recent name change for the one-time Department for Trade and Industry. A department that once upon a time used to have such an expressive, understandable and sensible name). Or perhaps even asking Trading Standards to intervene.

I'm not one to deny anyone a living (apart from the former PPI and current *'have you had an accident that wasn't your fault?'* hawkers), but it's just one more element in a succession of *'things'* (e.g. house buying in England, car wheel clamping) that seems to get heel-dragged until someone takes someone else to court to set a precedent. Either that or one of the consumer programmes on television or in the newspapers becomes involved.

But it shouldn't have to be that way!

Everyone complains so bitterly about the dysfunctionality of HR that something **must** surely be wrong. And it not just complaints because of the firing function power HR wields. Let's face it, someone has to be there to tell an employee their time is up if the employee is useless.

Sorry, I just had to get the current thoughts bit off my chest first.

Now, back to the beginning.

Chapter 3

HR was all the fault of an American gentleman. Well, being the bull it is, it would **have** to have been an American invention. Awesome. Wicked. Bad. And so on.

Yes, invented by those self-same people who put their luggage in the car trunk, diapers on babies, spend all their time *'reaching out'* (presumably they are lifeboat volunteers in their spare time) and who brought us the wonderful preposition *'pre'* that infests the English language with everything from the utterly meaningless *'pre-order'* (order before you order!) *'pre-owned'* (no, you dopes, it's second-hand or used) and the stupid *'pre-loved'*. In the same class as McDonalds French fries, but not as tasty, even with lashings of tomato ketchup.

I suppose it's to be expected that something as useless as HR should be invented in America, but in fairness, some mighty good inventions have come from America, and by and large, the Americans themselves are great people. Rather loud, yes, many are somewhat overweight and some do have the habit of dressing in very gaudy checked shirts that have the volume turned up to 11, but great people nevertheless.

Apart from the invention of all this HR nonsense stuff that is.

Anyway, you couldn't make this up.

The sadistic inventor who came up with this HR nonsense was a Frederick Winslow Taylor, and he was born in 1856 to a wealthy Quaker family in Germantown, Philadelphia, Pennsylvania.

And although nothing to do with HR, as an aside, an ancestor on his mother's side of the family was one of the fifteen original Mayflower Pilgrims.

He originally wanted to attend Harvard and become a lawyer, and despite passing the Harvard entrance examinations with honours in 1874, due to his failing eyesight, he became an apprentice pattern-maker and machinist.

Cynics like myself are of the somewhat considered opinion that this is extremely ironic given that HR would transform common sense into Health and Safety in the 1990's.

This meant that in order to empty your waste paper bin in the office, you now have to don your steel-toed safety boots, a high-visibility jacket and ask your fellow workers to stand back behind the *'Danger, wastepaper bin being emptied'* tape.

With failing eyesight, I would have thought working with heavy machinery would have been far riskier than studying in university, but hey, we're talking about setting the scene for the establishment of HR here. Working at something you are really not capable of. Or something you lack the facility for, and the ability in.

Or, perhaps I'm being unfair to suggest that if you have failing eyesight, being armed with a pair of suitable reading glasses so that you can quietly study a book sitting behind a desk might be far less dangerous that operating dangerous machinery.

But then, that's just my opinion. And I'm not an alleged HR expert.

Yes, we are, after all, talking about the founding father of the wild, wacky and wonderful world of HR, and what better than someone with acknowledged failing eyesight starting anew with industrial machinery.

It's a real HR sort-of thing to do! Health and Safety and burial ceremonies go well together.

Learning his trade, he moved up the *'corporate ladder'* (I cannot ascertain whether he had to don his steel-toed safety boots and high-visibility jacket to do this) at a couple of firms in Philadelphia, and his fast step-up was not alone just talent-based, but with the assistance of family connections.

After all, it's not what you know but who you know.

It was while at the Midvale Steel Works, complete with his failing eyesight, that he shoved his first HR oar in, noticing (I thought he had failing eyesight) that the workers were neither working themselves, nor their machines, to their full capacity.

In fairness, this is not altogether that bad an observance, because when all said and done, companies do have a right to expect their workers to do a fair day's work for a fair day's pay. Similarly, if it was stated by the car salesman that your car will attain 55mpg, you are hardly likely to be very pleased if after three months of ownership, you have never managed more than 25mpg, despite coasting down any road incline you come across.

By 1893, he'd moved into consulting, although it's probably fair to say that at the time, his brand of consulting was possibly a little more altruistic than its modern-day heavily-commissioned and bank-deposit driven equivalent, the type each successive government fails to learn from, despite being taken for a total ride time and time again. He spent the next five years perfecting his *'management and training systems'*. Quite a length of time, to be fair.

He gained fame, and to a degree, his fortune, as he continued to promote his management and machine-shop capacity-increasing methods, through lecturing, writing, and consulting.

To be fair to the man, what he primarily wanted to do was to simply improve industrial efficiency. This is not too bad an altruism. He was, after all, the first to systematically observe and study working practices, and to that end, he is considered the inventor of scientific management. And it was before the current crop of HR mandarins got their hands on their clipboards and never-ending sheets of coloured paper. And their very silly systems with stupid names.

Not forgetting a healthy dose of ring-fencing, blue sky thinking and envelope pushing.

HR has meandered a long way down the road to dysfunctional ruin since Taylor's original (and in actual fact, really somewhat logical) four principles of scientific management were introduced to the world.

These principles, which are actually quite sensible and really can't be argued against, are:

- The replacement of *'finger in the wind'* work methods with those based on a more scientific study of the tasks involved. He must be turning in his grave with the urine-to-the-wind methods employed by his current-day contemporaries.
- Select, train, and develop each employee in a more scientific and methodological manner, rather than doing nothing and letting them train or work things out for themselves – now replaced by the humble bum-lick in large corporations, where the face fitting is vitally more important than being better qualified to do the job in order to climb the corporate ladder with much more ease, simply because those in control are young and totally useless. Or telling people to gen up on-line.
- Provide *a 'detailed instruction and supervision of each worker in the performance of that worker's discrete task'* (Montgomery 1997: 250). Now this comprises of the usually, predictable copy-and-pasted *'evaluation form'* that the employee dutifully fills in and which then sits in an HR filing cabinet never to see the light of day ever again.

- Divide work nearly equally between managers and workers, so that the managers apply recognised and almost scientific management principles to planning the work while the workers actually perform required tasks they have been suitable trained and briefed to carry out. Yes, tell that to call-centre team leaders and managers.

And so, this became *'Taylorism'*, the first of many *'isms'* that have since followed their way into the wild and wacky world of HR over the years.

But what is perhaps most ironic of all is that were you to apply Taylor's principles of productivity and business net worth to HR departments throughout the land, the results would suggest that most of them should be dispensed with immediately.

Now, through his experience and observance of the humble worker, Taylor had quite precise ideas in his mind about how he would introduce his system. Jumping up and down in an infantile fashion on coloured squares at *a 'last Friday of the month'* happy-clappy HR bonding session had not yet been invented.

Although I'm sure the vital clipboard had been.

He felt that by standardising working methods, using the best tools for the job, providing good working conditions and making people cooperate with one another would ultimately produce faster, more accurate and higher quality work.

But achieving this was something management had to get their fingers out and do as well. Out of the window, then, with the company directors weekly Thursday golf outing and then using the Friday to recover.

And equally, no sitting back in a leather chair and awaiting the annual *'total lack of any perceivable contribution to the business but hey, we'll give you a wonderful bonus anyway'* bonus.

However, there was one aspect that would have had modern day unions up in arms. Taylor felt that workers were essentially stupid, totally incapable of either understanding what they were meant to do, or even comprehending the simplest of tasks. Not a very nice thing to say about the people who kept the business running and the directors and management in cigars and Malt Whiskey.

Like a true HR manager, he had already forgotten that he was once a raw recruit himself who needed coaching and training in his original chosen field of engineering. Even though he couldn't see a thing. He too would have at the time been totally incapable had he not been shown what to do. He felt that if someone was able to handle heavy metal (pig-iron), and was stupid enough to choose to do so for a living, he surely must have absolutely no comprehension of the science of the metal.

This is tantamount to accusing a modern-day bus driver of being unfit for the job because he has no clue as to how his engine works, or a domestic electrician has no idea how the local nuclear power station works.

And so, the HR rot was beginning to now set in, even before the term HR had been invented, or the useless institutes worldwide got their hands on it to turn it into a dysfunctional cash cow.

One could therefore perhaps be forgiven for thinking that any modern student of HR who reads the material written by Mr. Taylor would appear to be brainwashed at university into believing that on degree day, they would be heads and shoulders above their potential fellow members of staff

By the way, as an aside, check out the ingredients on a £3 bottle of Head and Shoulders – frighteningly similar to those of a £65 bottle of shampoo from one of the celebrity hairdressers.

And that's even before they start their new job of filling in time between pay days.

Using their clipboards.

But then, given the way the modern student happily takes in the fiction produced by the great unwashed of the National Union of Students as gospel, perhaps enough said!

One of his actions that particularly got up the noses of many workers as he went about creating his ideal *'them and us'* system - and thus set in stone the atmosphere in which many HR departments operate nowadays - was the transference of control from the workers to management, resulting in unrest and strikes.

He felt that comprehensive plans specifying the job and how it was to be done should be put together by management and communicated to the workers. And the modern equivalent can be seen very much in evidence in many businesses today.

This has resulted in clueless management, at the behest of equally, if not more so, clueless HR departments, issuing dysfunctional instructions, through lack of knowledge, to their otherwise modern-day highly-trained and quite competent workforce. Somewhat like the argument against university graduates entering the army or police directly as an officer without having done any basic training.

That some spotty oik fresh from university who doesn't know one end of a roll of toilet paper from the other should be issuing instructions to someone with both twenty years' experience and a naturally high competence and skill set for their job, seems to completely pass over their heads.

Taylor was of the not-unreasonable opinion that a worker worthy of being hired by him should have his pay linked to his productivity.

Fair enough. And in fact, his own workers actually earned more than other workers in other firms working under conventional management methods. So much so that the owners of factories who didn't use these *'scientific'* methods of running their businesses were very unhappy bunnies indeed.

Now, one of the upshots of this was that the restrictions on output that had up to then been the union's most dubious and disliked modus operandi would be broken. Taylor's response to give his methods some credibility was to say that there had never been a strike at a plant using his methods of scientific management.

It was thought he was perhaps being a little bit mythical, something modern HR people excel a lot at to this day.

He didn't actually produce a single shred of evidence that his methods reduced, as he claimed, working hours. So, HR people being inveterate fibbers isn't a modern-day aspect of HR at all! It's been around for decades!

Although Taylor was by no means whiter than white, he wasn't a total quack.

This was despite the fact that his messages often necessitated the total clampdown on worker's opposition, of intimidation, or of any human motives or aspirations other than those his view of development could encompass. He had decided it was to be his way, or no way.

He was very much the work's management equivalent of a modern-day religious extremist, his sense of reality sometimes clouded by his determination to get people to see and do things his way. A bit Scientological.

Mr. Taylor also had a fascination with the clock. Not as one who watched it to see when the working day might be ending, but for time and motion study. His analysis of work was almost anal to the point of obsessive, quite convinced that he could find *'the best way'*, that it, his ideal, the *'Taylor way',* for workers to do things.

He used to break down a job into its various constituent parts and make measurements of each to the hundredths of a minute.

The mind boggles than someone who was shovelling iron ore should have their job broken down into hundredths of a minute, but hey, we are after all talking about the birth of HR here! And yes, a hundredth of a minute is very measurable on the average 60-seond-to-a-minute scale. But as I said before, hey, this is the wild and wacky world of HR we're discussing here.

Yes, his most famous study was about shovels. As legendary Irish folk singer Christy Moore once sang, *'don't forget your shovel if you want to go to work'.*

But, no. Dear Christy had nothing on our Mr. Taylor. He noticed (Mr Taylor and not Christy), as any good HR person worth the air they breathe would, that workers in his industry used the same shovel for all materials.

That is, when they weren't leaning on one, smoking a cigarette and discussing the early 20th Century's equivalent of the tabloid page three girl in the newspaper shoved down the back of their trousers.

He discovered that the most effective load for a shovel was 21 ½ lbs., or 9.2kg. He then set about designing shovels that would scoop up precisely 21 ½ lbs. of various materials.

The one for 21 ½ lbs. of feathers or cotton wool was presumably the size of the average dumper truck.

Now, because very senior bosses at Bethlehem Steel where he worked at the time couldn't get their heads around this rather unusual concept of producing bespoke shovels for various materials, he was fired - lock, stock and shovel.

However, he did manage to persuade some workers – those who were paid according to how much stuff they shovelled and subsequently produced – to take on board his advice about shovelling and to break down the way they shovelled into better-performed shovelling activity.

And it was all thanks largely to one of his devotees, Henry Laurence Gantt - he of the often abhorred and derided *'Gantt chart'*, so beloved by HR people who are devoted to baffling everyone with bull, rather than dazzling everyone with brilliance – that his shovelling ideas were being adopted by industry.

Chapter 4

And so, with all this appropriate shovelling, the foundations of the stuff that farmers shovel, all cleverly disguised as HR, was now well on the way to become the totally dysfunctional and overvalued garbage we all love and disrespect to this today.

While the past century since HR's invention has not been kind to the humble worker (although it has, without doubt, been kind to the hordes of HR people and the relative Institutes who have all these people as their paying membership), a little more about HR during these few intervening years must be made mention. Painful though it might be, I apologise to all those unfortunates amongst you who have, over the years, fallen victim to the dysfunctional HR nonsense, fabrication and often downright dishonesty and lies.

And similar apologies must be proffered to those HR people who are forthright, honest and genuinely good at their job. Those who insist on being called personnel managers and actually know what is going in the firms they work for. Those who are respected by their fellow workers, rather than derided by them.

It might not come as a surprise that a couple of very nice men, two of the Soviet Union's most cuddly and affable reality stars, Vladimir Lenin, together with his equally huggable strictly non-dancing partner Joseph Stalin, were both very impressed, as only dictators could be, by Taylorism.

'We must have this for our own manufacturing industries, Joey baby', Vlad was overheard whispering into Stalin's ear one evening when they were attending a reality TV-style, opposition-quashing murder session.

However, by now, the detractors were bubbling to the surface. And by no means was it just that they were jealous of Taylor's progress.

It was meanwhile, somewhere in Canada, a gentleman, Henry Mintzberg, was being a tad highly critical of our dear Mr. Taylor and his methods. He said something that will be close to the hearts of workers the world over who have to put up with insufferable HR practices in their workplace.

This was that an obsession with efficiency (admittedly an obsession that has not particularly bothered HR people in their own industry) can allow the benefits to smother some of the social benefits thus allowing social values to get cast aside.

Something to be borne in mind when the overpaid and dishonest TUPE (TUPE stands for Transfer of Undertakings [Protection of Employment] more of that later). A TUPE transfer happens when an organisation, or part of it, is transferred from one employer to another. Or when a service is transferred to a new provider, for example when another company takes over the contract for office cleaning. A consultant starts work in an office (not by any means that they are all dishonest or necessarily overpaid), obfuscating what is nothing more than a redundancy round disguised as a fluff-bunny exercise.

Another gentleman, James Rinehart said that using Taylor's methods to transfer production control from workers to management and then dividing that labour up into simple task units just annoys workers and can lead to workplace unrest as work.

While it becomes repeatable from a quality point of view, it also becomes totally monotonous and can be skill-reducing, especially where a worker has a more significant skill-set than that demanded by the re-aligned job.

Now, that covers, in a very broad outline, the invention of HR as a single, useless and dysfunctional entity.

The history of human resource/personnel management (HRM) and human resource development (HRD) differ slightly to the actual HR process itself, and were around as a *'generalist'* management function somewhat before Frederick Winslow Taylor appeared on the scene.

It was he who simply spun it a little more scientifically. This was also before the pseudo-academics of the *'industry'* invented the actual *'Human Resource'* label itself.

At the back end of the 19th Century, when it all began, it was simply called personnel management. It was at this time that welfare officers - sometimes called welfare secretaries - came into being. These were all women and were very much involved solely with the protection of women and girls.

It was all part of a reaction to the brutality of working conditions in industry and the pressures that were then being brought to bear to improve those awful conditions. Not such a bad thing at all, if truth be told.

The labour movement and trade unions were beginning to exert pressure.

Some of the more humane and open employers, in particular the Quakers, were starting to honourably shove their oar in with regards to improving conditions and recognising the worth of the employee more as a business asset rather than a business tool.

However, there still were those who couldn't quite get their head around the fact there might be a moral obligation to protect women and children rather than sacrifice greater output and larger profits.

Then the unexpected arrived that was to change everything.

The First World War.

This was an altogether real game-changer as far as employment and equality were concerned.

For the first time in history, women were helping to take the place of men who had trundled off to war. And that meant things had to be worked out with the unions, who weren't all that keen on replacing those skilled men with unskilled women.

That it never entered the union's heads while the men were off saving the country, the women could actually be taught and trained was nothing but the totally simplistic and chauvinistic mind-set at the time!

Onwards and forwards into the 1920's, and as the world recovered from the war, the larger factories in industry started to create employment or labour managers to look after aspects relating to employment - all the stuff current HR people mismanage from their ivory towers. Hiring, dismissal, bonuses, absence, clipboards etc.

After the 1929 financial crash and onwards into the recovering 1930's, as things began to pick up, the owners of emerging newer industries, not yet having the wool pulled over their eyes by useless HR directors (or using them as their cowardly way out of dealing with their own employees), saw the benefits of treating their employees like human beings.

They saw the good in offering encouragement and incentive to employ, motivate and keep their workers. Employees were at last beginning to be seen as an investment rather than just a throwaway commodity.

Full-time working dedicated personnel people came into their own with the outbreak of the Second World War, in particular for those companies manufacturing war materials. Not only did the edict come directly from the Government recognising the need for welfare workers in munitions factories, but the Ministry of Labour and National Service, now somewhat expanded, insisted on this being the case.

By 1945, the whole employment management and welfare work thing was now seen as being under the broad term *'personnel management'*, although at the time, very far removed from its modern-day dysfunctional and sometimes quite corrupt equivalent.

However, it was all experiential in as much as how logical it may sound to us all nowadays. It was the war that had very much demonstrated productivity and subsequently output of finished *'goods'* could be influenced by employment policies.

So, while modern day HR is indeed seen as being very bureaucratically driven, the image back then was of a very bureaucratic profession that was emerging.

The next major overhaul of the personnel business was at a time of industrial unrest and dreadful relations during the 1960's, and this was when Lord Donovan was instructed to head a Royal Commission to look into things.

His report, produced in 1968, slammed into employers and unions alike. He also had a go at personnel managers whose negotiating skills he felt were abysmal and whom he thought were clueless at planning industrial relations strategies.

He also thought that management simply wasn't giving personnel matters a high enough ranking on their to-do lists, or empowering personnel management to get on with the job.

This is all little different to the scene nowadays, where the new breed of HR management needs to actually be reeled in and the general management - and those at director level all the way up to chief executive - made play a much bigger part and be more hands-on in the affairs of their workers.

It was around the 1970's that the HR circus really arrived in town big time, laying the foundation for what has now become the single biggest dysfunctional financial drain on many a modern business - the HR department.

However, it's not all bad. Well nearly not all.

It wasn't until the mid-1980's that the term *'human resource management'* arrived, as only it could, in all its dysfunctional glory, from the USA. Only the Americans could think up something so fanciful, and only the British could follow so sheep-like in implementing all the brain-dead nonsense that came with it.

So, it was then full steam ahead for *'SS Bull'*, as personnel methodologies were developed that drew on theories from the social sciences about motivation and organisational behaviour.

Employers started to use a variety of assessment methods to define an applicant's suitability for a position, which is fair enough if they're individually personalised for the requirements of the job and not just copied and pasted from some useless HR lip-service website.

And these assessment methods included the nirvana of HR bull, the unbelievably incomprehensible and completely inconclusive waste of time that is ……… the psychometric test (unless, of course, you are on a medical prescription and need to have your *'psychomets'* checked regularly).

Yes, more about these puerile quizzes later. (If you want to have a go at some of these tests, take a look at https://www.practiceaptitudetests.com/psychometric-tests or for short, shorturl.at/pCO57, or failing that, do check out some of the old Monty Python sketches on YouTube).

Now as these assessment methods - in fairness, some good, as well those that are totally useless - came more into practice, management training started to expand. Again, some of these were good, others unbelievably useless, yet this didn't prevent the management consultants multiplying in their thousands like a bad rash and getting on the road in their 7-Series BMW's to rake in fortunes expounding what was (and certainly is even more so nowadays) often complete and utter overvalued and overpaid garbage.

The infuriating term *'human resources'* is nothing if not an interesting one. While it might appear on the outside to infer employee commitment and motivation, that's precisely what the HR wallahs would like we mere mortals' take on it to be.

It actually suggests that workers are an asset or resource-like machine.

The modern-day HR *'profession'* now includes a number of disciplines, including diversity, reward (compensation, benefits and pensions), resourcing, employee relations, organisation development and design, and learning and development.

However, it's all really nothing a competent administrator couldn't undertake, providing all the accompanying smoke-screen flannel is stripped out. HR is really the equivalent of a Mercedes AMG 63, but with a Ford 900cc engine installed to run it, thus allowing relatively inexperienced teenagers to drive it.

The CIPD offers members a self-assessment tool to assess capability against the *'Profession Map'* to identify gaps in knowledge and behaviours. This supposedly provides recommendations that can be used to create a bespoke learning plan tailored to personal development needs and aspirations.

Whatever all that means.

More flannel of course. But hey, it brings in a few extra pounds.

Chapter 5

And so to the subtle difference between human resource management (HRM) and human resource development (HRD).

HRD is rather more about training - or at least it's meant to be, were it not peddled now by the HR merchants. It was originally conceived in response to the late 19th Century's concern in Government circles about the poor standard of Britain's labour force compared with other industrialised nations. There was justifiable worry about a potential lack of competitiveness as a result of this lacking on the part of UK plc.

As I said, all very plausible, well-intentioned and very necessary. And there can be no denying that a well-trained workforce remains extremely vital for the UK's (and for that matter any country's) continued commercial success.

But not in the destructive and self-obsessive hands of the HR department wallahs as it is now. In an organisation serious about worker training and development, it needs to be assigned its own department well away from HR and placed firmly in the charge of people who are well-trained and experienced themselves - and not just with an irrelevant or transferred university degree.

It needs people who actually know what they are doing.

And unlike HR, they actually know what actual part in the success of the business the people they are training play. Together with the actual function they are paid to carry out.

It may seem harsh, but so many of the average HR wallahs really do not appear to know what their fellow worker does.

The First World War was one of the first of the planet's highly-mechanised international conflicts, and as such, needed the extremely quick supply of arms and ammunition. In the UK, the Ministry of Munitions got off its civil service backside and devised a series of training programmes which had the specific aim of producing trained machine operators in 90 days.

Then, in 1917, as the aftermath of the conflict started to gain momentum, the training shifted nobly towards the many disabled ex-servicemen to help them gain both jobs and trade union membership.

Following the end of hostilities, the Government started to give priority to potential skill shortages, while at the same time thinking about reducing mass unemployment.

By 1925, the Interrupted Apprenticeship Scheme was back on track for those whose apprentices had originally been *'interrupted'* by the war. There were also training schemes established for women.

All these schemes had the enthusiastic aim of relieving long-term unemployment, but by the end of the 30's and the onset of the Second World War, normality went out the window with the *'all hands-on deck'* call.

By the time the Second World War was coming to a close, courses were again started, this time the training being focused on the needs of the building industry to help rebuild Britain.

But, with the best will and intention in the world, the quality of this particular training was considered the lighter side of dreadful. Yes, as a result of the war, there was still no marked change in attitude towards formal training.

With the full employment period that followed the war, it was felt that employers should really take charge of training their employees, although this was taken to mean apprenticeships that were time-served.

These apprenticeships, and the training that went with them, was allied to the individual industry.

But then the 1970's arrived, and with it, brought a rise in unemployment, with various schemes being developed to train young people in an effort to get them off the streets from doing nothing and into gainful activity.

One particular scheme to help unemployed 16-18-year-old school leavers gain work experience through training and preparation courses was the often-derided Youth Opportunities Programme (YOP).

This began in 1978 under the Labour Government, lead at the time by James Callaghan, and was expanded in 1980 by Margaret Thatcher's Conservative Government. It ran until 1983, when it was replaced by the Youth Training Scheme (YTS).

1987 saw the establishment of the National Council for Vocational Qualifications (NCVQ) scheme to bring a new vocational qualification framework (slightly different in Scotland with an 'S' preceding everything) and structure to qualifications, which included recognition accreditation for what had already been learned and accomplished.

In 1989, Training and Enterprise Councils (TECs) arrived in England and Wales, again slightly different in Scotland and Northern Ireland where they were Local Enterprise Companies (LECs). They had the aim of making training bespoke to the needs of the local population and had full control over the funding given to them by the Government.

The only problem was that many were staffed at the top end by at times rather clueless senior civil servants who had never been in the commercial world before (but whom, with Employment Service [now called DWP] experience, in fairness, were often very good at the non-real-world end of things relating to the paper-shuffling for employment).

There were also a number of other organisations peddling the same help (information and signposting, that is) offered at the time by the TECs.

That having been said, the TECs did a really quite good job (except for the solitary one of the 82 of them that was struck off), but as is the case with any new incumbent Government, the TECs were an easy target for a quick tit-for-tat *'get-rid'* that stamped their disapproval on the previous work of the ousted government.

Tits for tat, so to speak.

This type of pettiness generally causes the downfall of some initiative or other following a change of political administration, in this case from Conservative to Labour (the Conservatives got their own back 20 years later by getting rid of the Labour-installed Development Agencies when the Conservatives assumed power in May 2010).

It's like each new incoming Government has to always make some childish and churlish stand, without any reference to the consequences of their actions, just to prove they are in power and the previous lot may have, in their opposing eyes, made a mess. It's OK for well-salaried parliamentarians. They have a guaranteed 5-year gravy train and magnificent pension if they are thrown out by their electorate.

Forward to 2003, and the skills strategy paper issued by the Government which by now aimed to help employers gain the skills they needed to succeed in their business as well as to ensure that employees had the skills to be employable.

They wanted to integrate skills and ensure that everyone around - employer, worker and man in the street - played their part in focusing on the future for a skilled Britain.

In theory, a wonderful idea, but omitting to factor-in the consultants and other parasites and leeches waiting in the wings to pounce on all the Government money sloshing around so that they could have it sloshing around in their own bank accounts instead.

The Leitch Review was then tasked in 2004 with considering the UK's long-term skills needs. Following a little think, a little tank and then a little scribble, the good Lord published his final report on a Tuesday, namely, 5 December 2006.

Niftily titled *'Prosperity for all in the Global Economy: World Class Skills'* it looked at the UK's long-term skills needs and powered ahead setting a target for the country to reach a set skill level by 2020 that would dumbfound the remainder of the civilised world with how fantastic the UK would become. A jolly good intention, to be honest.

Not content with merely this as a goal, m'Lud followed it up in 2006 with a Review of Skills. This aimed to chip away more efficiently at the low skill levels in the UK and head towards the majority of the population having at least a Level 2 Qualification (GSCE with grades C-A or equivalent). It also intended for employers to support this by voluntarily committing to train their workers to this level. In fairness, thoroughly laudable.

A few years later though, for young people and those without basic skills, the Government had since kicked this into touch, and now relies more, at the time of writing, on apprenticeships. Skills development is a critical aspect of HRD, but the neglect of what goes on within the workforce is certainly one of the major failings of policy in recent years.

Now, back to the CIPD - the Chartered Institute of Personnel and Development. When it started back in 1913, it had a proper name that people could relate to - the Welfare Workers' Association (WWA). Unlike today, with its 160,000 paying members, it had just 34 people, 29 of whom were women. It was all related to a concern for welfare at work and the working conditions of female employees in factories.

So, while its modern-day equivalent may think it is *'championing better work and better lives'*, its origins were altogether very much humbler. No fancy Broadway address in Wimbledon then, neither was there an income of £38.6 million (for the year 2020-2021, with, at the time of writing, an annual membership being £238 for a Chartered Member and an administrative charge of £40 as well as any assessment fee required to achieve membership).

Neither were there any chief executives paying themselves the absolute fortune of a six-figure annual salary and bonus (Bonus? Whatever for? Fiddling as Rome burns more-like) in excess of twice the salary of the Prime Minister. But more of that later.

Back in 1916, which any good, on-the-ball, qualified HR manager will tell you is a minute past a quarter-past seven, any concern controlled by the Ministry that employed people had to appoint its own welfare workers, and towards the end of the war, about 1,000 had been appointed, some 600 of them members of the WWA.

At the same time, more men were now being recruited as *'Labour Officers'*, particularly those who had experience of shop floor life, to help with the likes of recruitment, discipline, dismissal and industrial relations at plant management level amongst unionised male workers. There were problems concerning workers' rights as they were dismissed from work in connection with Munitions Tribunals following the war.

The WWA then went through a period of name changing during the seven years from 1917-1924, and that was before the advent of the modern brand image agency charging a fortune just to add an expensive squiggle and a change of typeface to an existing logo. Ker-ching, £50,000 please.

Sensibly, it was a response to the various welfare associations that had sprung up nationwide, and the main WWA didn't want the movement to splinter. Sensible thinking.

So, it was renamed the Central Association of Welfare Workers (CAWW) in 1917, and by 1924, it had again changed name, this time to the Institute of Industrial Welfare Workers (IIWW) by 1924.

Unfortunately, labour officers and managers didn't appear to appreciate the focus on welfare that the IIWW seemed to have, and very few joined it. And it didn't help that those who had held more senior positions in their own organisations would have been expected to essentially downgrade to join the IIWW.

A classic case of the chiefs wanting to remain chiefs and not become Indians, even if it was for the benefit of the masses.

Nothing much has changed in that regard with anything, not just HR throughout the world over the years!

So, all these labour management people became, whether by accident or by design, connected, with the all chiefs and no Indians intention of forming their own separate association. In 1931, the IIWW once again changed its name, this time to the Institute of Labour Management (ILM) in an attempt to mirror the changing nature of the function.

Even its journal, *'Welfare Work'* changed its name to *'Labour Management'*.

Then, in 1946, the Institute changed its name to the Institute of Personnel Management as the era of quite full-employment in the years post war meant personnel work began to expand.

By 1955, things had ramped up, and the Institute headed towards allowing full membership only if you passed the examination.

Not necessarily a bad thing.

At the same time, it introduced a scheme whereby external colleges could run courses to *'prepare'* students for the exam. Naturally enough, despite being long before the era of Rip-Off Britain of the 90's, this set in motion a mushrooming of colleges and institutions who would begin to offer personal management courses. Not for free, you will of course appreciate.

In 1994, the Institute of Personnel and Development then *'happened'* following the merger of the Institute of Personnel Management (IPM) with the Institute of Training and Development (ITD).

As the hip saying goes, then the two became one.

Or maybe I'm confusing things with the Spice Girls.

The first thing the newly formed Institute set about was securing the vital condition called *'chartered status'*.

The original IPM had been banging on about this for a while prior to the merger, and it was duly chartered in 2000, and the CIPD as we know, love and deride it, came into existence on the 1 July of that year.

Then on 1 October 2003, the CIPD awarded chartered status to over 37,000 full Members, Fellows and Companions of the Institute.

By now, HR and all that accompanies the modern-day version was ramping up at an altogether breakneck and ever-more alarming rate, and in 2009, the CIPD's *'Profession Map'* was launched (yes, I have checked my atlas and it appears there isn't a country call *'Profession'*). This map is meant to be a *'dynamic and live'* (somewhat of an oxymoron when it comes to HR) set of standards, quite remarkable really, seeing its origins are from people – and for people – many of whom could not necessarily be accused of being the most dynamic people in the world of business.

So, a question many ask, is a degree really necessary to be an HR professional?

Well, personally, it depends on how you might think of a profession. Being a market-trader is classed as a profession, as is driving a bus, running a taxi or selling newspapers. Each has its own level of professionalism, with most involving an element of some training or other, especially in the case of where you are charged with ensuring fellow humans are safe as you go about your job. Driving a bus could be learned by observation, but you do need a hefty element of official training, a double-dose of sheer ability and the official DVLA rubber-stamping of your permission to drive that bus.

But you don't need a degree. Despite having the lives of your passengers in your hands every minute of the day you are driving that bus.

Dipping into Oxford's finest word book, one finds the definitions of profession are:

- a vocation requiring knowledge of some department of learning or science: the profession of teaching
- any vocation or business
- the body of persons engaged in an occupation or calling: to be respected by the medical profession.

Now HR, no matter how we may view it from a practical point of view, is most definitely an occupation rather than a profession. This is regardless of whether we think of it as a hazard (that is, an occupational hazard) or otherwise.

But even the most active of brains could not classify it as a *'learned'* profession, such as medicine or engineering. Yes, those professions, and others, require that the holder has a recognised degree to prove they have the relevant learning and knowledge to *'practice'* their professionalism, particularly if it has an impact on peoples' safety and lives.

Now while I have a couple of degrees myself (and a fat lot of use they have proven, thanks largely to HR, over the latter years!), they do not entitle me to perform brain surgery, to put up a suspension bridge over the river Thames or to manage the accounts of the Acme Company of Bristol. Neither do my degrees enable me to drive a bus or to become a firefighter.

However, I could become an HR director. Which would be far better, somewhat easier and much more financially rewarding and empowered than having to work for a living.

And while many of the bright young things coming out of business schools with the HR degrees may be the ones now being engaged in personnel jobs all over, they, and their profession continue to garner less respect than the average serial killer.

Yet there certainly are many HR people who are respected for who they are, what they do, the effort they put in to their job and the educated and knowledgeable manner they go about their work.

Take the three people I mentioned in my preamble at the beginning of this book. Three extremely professional and able HR people in three very differing industries.

But there are so many of these HR workers who haven't, and won't receive any recognition whatsoever, no matter how hard they go at it, because their career path has already been blighted by those before them. They are just lowly *'HR staff'*. Condemned to a life of pen-pushing and photocopying unless they make strides to better themselves.

And no amount of *'chartering'* or *'certification'* will help, unless those heading the profession take their overpaid heads out of the sand and do something about cleaning up their act. And making it less of an act to boot!

HR has to gain the respect of the common worker, prove its worth, and be seen not just simply as the stick for cowardly CEOs and directors to beat their staff with.

And by so doing, it might even shake off the mantle of being referred to as *'Human Remains'* or the *'Business Prevention Unit'*.

There is the argument that until they are all degreed, HR will never be referred to as a profession. Wrong! When it becomes more professional, then it will be referred to as a profession. It's as simple as that. Respect has to be earned and not bullied upon people.

At the moment, HR is the business equivalent of allowing the lunatics to run the asylum.

It should be that like medicine, law and teaching, where you can't simply fall into HR as a profession should you see it as an easy out to get you to your pension. Managing people shouldn't be carried out in the haphazard, finger-to-the wind fashion that is has on many occasions been.

But it must be remembered that having a degree does not automatically grant you professional status! And this applies to all walks of business life, not just HR.

I am sure there are plenty of lousy solicitors, teachers and even, sadly, doctors, just like there are many lousy HR people.

But the latter are more obvious because of the reputation of the overall HR and recruitment industry as a whole. It has been well and truly tarred with a brush lacking bristles.

Ok, I appreciate this whole HR business goes a little deeper than that. Very few solicitors, teachers or doctors have been described by their *'customers'* as a laughing stock.

If you are taken for a ride by your bank, you have the Financial Conduct Authority as a back-up to help you. If you fall foul of a TUPE and you never see the CEO's backside for dust during the entire exercise, you might as well go outside and try to tinkle against the wind hoping your clothes won't get wet unless you have a shedload of money to chuck at an employment law specialist, seeing as the guilty in HR are so speedy with their gagging orders.

So, in an attempt, painful though it is when it comes to anything to do with HR, for me to be a little less facile and cut the HR bods some slack, I will note that it has been created by the *'profession'* for the *'profession'* and is meant to benchmark successful and effective HR helping those responsible to deliver across every aspect and specialism of the HR *'profession'*. It's just a great shame that HR itself is has become so weak, useless and by and large, totally dysfunctional and completely unprofessional. Not to mention, derided and hated by all - bar those employed in it - who come into contact with it.

To come more up to date, I've already mentioned that today, at the time of writing, the CIPD has over 160,000 members internationally, all engaged in HR, people management, learning, development and consulting.

And it cannot be denied that it is the oldest professional HR association in the world. Although it is, to a degree, somewhat overshadowed by the Society for Human Resource Management in the Unites States of America, which is the largest professional association dedicated to HR. It has over 250,000 members in some 140 countries.

But that is down to relative populations and sheer numbers. And the Americans do love their bull.

And yes, the CIPD do research, lobby, inform and shape. In their own way. And in fairness, they do attempt to find better pathways into work for those seeking a job. Like any organisation, regardless of how poor it might be overall, I cannot deny there are indeed some fantastic professionals in the CIPD doing an altogether excellent job.

Chapter 6

Moving back to America for a moment, you may be interested - although I was shocked - to learn that there are over half a million HR practitioners in the United States.

Over there, being an HR manager consistently ranks as one of the best jobs in a company, and is it any wonder? No pressure to sell or contribute to the bottom-line profit of an organisation.

If you're hiring, but are especially useless, you can bring in help from an outside recruiter with absolutely no questions asked while still retaining your full salary. Not bad eh? Getting a full salary to sub-contract out your daily work.

Could you image the outcry if a member of parliament left everything to their secretary to do, including trying to solve constituents' problems, kissing snotty babies at election time and voting in parliament!

Or if you were a car salesman having difficulty making sales. Being able to bring in an outsider to do all the work so you could sit back and push your pen around your notepad and spend the day merrily posting pictures of your meals and your cat on Instabook and Facegram, yet at the same time still receiving your full salary and your commission on each car sale.

Nice one.

Yes, the one industry that is outsourced regularly despite having some senior in situ, on a rather healthy salary, who, in reality, if they are such a professional and so needed, they should really be doing the job themselves. Nice lack of work if you can get it! And it doesn't stop there.

Time now to have a peek at what these merchants do in the modern, current world. The textbooks say that the primary objectives of the HR manager should be:

1. Health and safety of the workforce
2. Development of a superior workforce
3. Development of the Human Resources department
4. Development of an employee-oriented company culture that emphasises quality, continuous improvement, key employee retention and development, and high performance
5. Personal ongoing development.

So, let's have a quick look each of these objectives one-by-one.

Health and safety of the workforce

Well, this is right up the average HR manager's alleyway, as it involves plenty of jobs worthiness, shed-loads of paper work, plenty of certificates, reviews, case-studies, the hiring of consultants and, most importantly, a clipboard.

Long before health and safety, each company had a specialist initiative in place called common sense. And not just in the workplace. For example, if your work involved a motorcycle, you wore a helmet and suitable protective clothing, on the off-chance that you might either fall off said motorcycle, or it might rain.

If you were a bricklayer, you made sure you had steel-capped boots and a hard hat, as wearing flip-flops meant that should you drop a brick on your foot, you would have to use rather expletive and coarse language out loud.

And a cloth cap, even if a northern-based bricklayer, does not cut the mustard for a brick landing on your head. As well as taking that copy of the Sun newspaper out from the back of your trousers so as to allow you to lie down on the ambulance stretcher.

And if you were a zoo-keeper, you know it wouldn't necessarily be the height of sensibility to cook and eat your steak lunch inside the lion enclosure without a safety harness.

Now the way health and safety and its issues has wandered off the common-sense track is not really the fault of HR people.

Because, bearing in mind the job they do, the health and safety people can be mind-bogglingly stupid all on their own, without any assistance or intervention from HR or anyone else for that matter.

For example, students at their graduation ceremony at Anglia Ruskin University in Cambridge were told not to pose for pictures throwing their hats in the air in case someone was injured by the hats falling back to earth. The reason for this was that someone had been hurt by a falling hat a few years previously.

There's none so blind as those who refuse to see.

Another health and safety joy left the Mayor of Maidstone, in Kent, southern England, extremely upset when the flag bearing the town crest was forcibly removed from her official mayoral car, as council officials felt that the flag breached rules.

It was said that the flag could be a hazard to both drivers and pedestrians if it fell off. They even claimed it would reduce the value of the car. Personally, I won't even entertain the thought of buying a car without a mayoral flag. But in fairness to the health and safety people, mayoral flags can be anything up to 16cm x 9cm in size and weight anything up to 100g, i.e. the size and weight of an A5 piece of card. Very much a danger to . . . ants.

Take care Adam, there's a rampant mayoral flag about being chased after by a council official from Maoidstone.

And June Turnbell, a sprightly 79-year-old pensioner from Wiltshire, proudly supported her local village by tending a council-owned flower bed for several years. Not only that, but she also spent hundreds of pounds of her own money on plants and garden tools.

But this wasn't good enough for health and safety-obsessed council officials.

They decided, in their wisdom – or as we mortals call it, abject stupidity - that her efforts breached safety rules because of a bend in the road beside the plot, and that in order to continue with her self-funded civic volunteering, she would have to put up *'Men at work'* signs, wear a fluorescent jacket and even employ a look-out.

Then, presumably, an irate and increasingly litigious public would be demanding their money back because Australian rockers (they were actually led by a Scotsman, Colin James Hay) *'Men at Work'* did a no show.

Presumably the Health and Safety profession has its own equivalent pop hit, but with the chorus line *'I come from a land down Blunder'*.

Keep death off the road and drive on the flowerbed.

Even the Health and Safety Executive themselves are not totally immune to their own stupidity.

Staff were banned from moving chairs around in case they hurt themselves, and anyone wanting to move furniture had to book a porter to do it, with 48 hours' notice.

I even had the same total inanity myself at a company I worked for.

I had to load up the contents of my desk and filing cabinet (containing loads of dangerous pieces of paper and very heavy staplers, hole punchers and ball point pens) into three crates, wait patiently for '*office services*' to arrive with a trolley (having patiently sat around for two hours after the time they promised they would arrive) to move them all the way to the desk facing me.

It was deemed a serious hazard to my health for me to move my stuff across the desk to the adjoining one opposite myself.

Next, they'll be telling international rugby players to gently place the ball at the goal line rather than throw themselves at it in so as to avoid potentially bruising their knees.

Development of a superior workforce

This is really like the BBC saying it is dedicated to developing a superior reality (sorry, should I be pronouncing that '*ree-al-ihy*'?) show. If you haven't the suitable participants - or the willing staff in the case of a company - don't expect the incredible. Yes, all companies want to be better than their competitors. It's only natural.

But if you are blessed with the average Herbert who is covered in tattoos, pierced with rivets through his ears and temples, lives and breathes football and just wants to work in order to just get paid, he probably is quite happy doing as best as he can to ensure he maintains that pay and keeps the management happy.

He will have no interest whatsoever in taking part in activities to do with *'developing a superior workforce'* if there's nothing tangible and highly rewarding in it for him! Why should he worry that the MD wants to replace executive car? It's of no material gain to Herbert what car the MD drives.

Give him an extra few hundred quid a month and he might be a more willing victim.

Development of the Human Resources department

Well, yes. If there's one thing that the average HR head is capable of, it's protecting their own. Divide and multiply. At any expense. In fact, the HR department in many a business is the only one that seems to breed without any form of consensual business-generating co-habitation being necessary for its reproduction.

I remember a very good friend of mine who worked for an international bank in Canary Wharf, London. It was around the time of the 2008/2009 banking crisis when in order to avoid any senior banking executives facing the chop and losing their huge salaries and bonuses, they decided to get rid of the workers instead. Remember, the workers are the ones who do the real work, earn the money for the bank and serve the customers.

This friend worked on an upper floor that was half-empty, and in order to get rid of the staff, the half-empty bit was suddenly overflowing with HR merchants. Yes, those members of staff in a bank who contributes absolutely zero to its profitability.

The ones who don't help customers, who doesn't operate 24-hour banking services, who don't fix errant cash machines, the one who don't try an prevent bank fraud or money laundering, the ones who don't qualify business loans.

There the ones who don't even flog over-priced house insurance, in fact, the ones who don't even stuff a customer letter into an envelope.

As an aside, I wonder what the Health and Safety people make of workers travelling to and from Canary Wharf aboard the Docklands Light railway with its driverless trains?

Yes, I know, I'm now being even more facile than usual.

So really, if looked at intelligently, with a degree of strategy thrown in, HR people should be more involved with developing the company rather than themselves, because by developing themselves they are actually doing nothing for the company they work for or producing any sales or turnover.

More importantly, they are doing nothing for the employee whose welfare they are allegedly meant to also be looking after.

Taking a look at the Irish banking crisis and recession of 2008 – 2011. Now here was an absolute country-load of HR people, not just fiddling while Rome crashed and burned, but playing an entire symphony and several follow-up concerts.

According to Shane Ross (an independent Irish parliamentarian) and Nick Web (business editor of the Sunday Independent newspaper), it was revealed back in 2011 in their book *'The Untouchables'*, (https://www.amazon.co.uk/Untouchables-Shane-Ross/dp/0241956242 or shorturl.at/puAP9) during one of the worst recessions in modern Irish history, that the average salary at the National Treasury Management Agency (borrows money on behalf of Ireland from international markets) had risen to €100,000, with a bonus pot of €2million. Fourteen staff at the agency were pulling in more than €250,000 a year.

Remember, the Irish banking system was not even remotely clear of the its crashing and burning of the previous three years. HR? Ain't life grand?

Or as the 14 above will agree, 250 grand.

In 2007, the year before everything financial came crashing down in the Republic, a fancy HR *'Performance Management and Development System'* had been introduced into the Irish Civil Service. 17,728 officials were tested on *a '1 means no pay increase'* to *'5 means the sun shines out of your ass'*, with no mechanism whatsoever in place for sacking.

Now, bearing in mind the country was already well on the way to becoming a third-world basket case, this grading system, dreamt up by some HR consultants, produced the following:

9 staff scored a 1 – *'denial of salary increase'*
172 scored a 2 – *'needs improvement'*

The remainder of the 17,728 – that's 17,547 were good performers (3), exceeding expectations (4) or outstanding (5). So, while the country was falling asunder and starting its run to the world bank to be bailed out, HR in the civil service running the country was all tickety-boo, with thousands of civil service people getting pay increases.

And not only that, but in successive years, as the country went so far to the dogs it made Robert Mugabe's style of country management look rational, the number of civil servants improving their scores rose. This included the Department for Finance people who seemed totally unaware that Ireland was going down the financial toilet.

To be sure, to be sure, ain't HR just really grand?

HR people the world over it seems are all great at rewarding and/or supporting failure while at the same time have equal, if not greater expertise at empire building.

And that leads nicely to the next *'objective'*.

Development of an employee-oriented company culture that emphasises quality, continuous improvement, key employee retention and development, and high performance

Now forgive me if I'm wrong, but this particular *'objective'* is, to put it rather proverbially, all backside over tip.

Yes, by all means, they should help with the development of an employee-oriented company culture, thereby do something of value for the company that is employing them.

But please, bring the key employee retention and development part more to the fore guys, for heaven's sake! Especially the retention bit. It costs a fortune to employ and train a new worker.

This activity is also a bit of a cop-out for the chief executive, managing director or whoever owns the company.

They themselves - and by all means by taking advice - should be moulding the company into what they perceive to be the best way to run it. After all, the owner is meant to be the supposed chief honcho for expertise in running the business.

They should be constantly monitoring what's going on in their own company. They should be ensuring the quality. Yes, by all means use the services of someone with expertise in the company to do that, but don't all take both your eyes, ears and entire body from the company ball yourselves guys!

However, the above having been said, the company owner or directors shouldn't start getting a bad case of supervision addiction, letting others do all the donkey work. Because if you use donkeys, they sure as hell will pull the company cart in the best direction of the carrot.

And the converse is also true.

Don't insist on doing absolutely everything yourself either.

Unless you are the extremely talented multi-instrumentalist Roy Wood, you don't play all the instruments in your rock group yourself!

And so on.

Personal ongoing development

By now, whether the HR people have run out of objectives, or whether it's a space-filling exercise, we come to the bull-deluxe of objectives.

The make-it-up-as-you-go-along objective. The one that would make the landed aliens pack up their spaceships and head back to Planet Zog.

This is the one particularly adored by the HR merchants. The Nirvana for the clip-board brigade. Because it can involve a whole host of external things.

Not to forget the rolling up of the sleeves and the total immersion in all the wonderful stuff that really doesn't benefit the business one, single iota.

But it does make the HR person seem very busy.

Which is vitally important, seeing as they don't otherwise directly contribute anything to the bottom-line profit of the business themselves.

It involves plenty of boring and totally meaningless PowerPoint presentations using words no one understands, expensive consultants coming into the business bringing plenty of facile and very expensive mushroom-growing (keep in the dark and feed with cow-dung) trashy and insulting memory tests with them. (I believe these are sometimes referred to as psychometric tests, which I have already referred to earlier). All stuff that tries the patience and turns workers even more against them.

It involves plenty of squares of coloured paper, trips to hotels, bonding sessions, teamwork, breakout sessions followed by plenary sessions (i.e. small groups in different places followed by everyone together in one room), copying and pasting from both American HR and the CIPD websites, the ordering of buffet lunches, plenty of printing and photocopying.

And plenty of dashing out of the room to make vital phone calls, mainly to whom we know not, because anyone they might need to phone during the work day is busy back in the room either jumping up and down on those wonderful coloured squares of paper or having their psychomets tested to the full.

But most importantly, it involves clipboards, one for each HR person, as well as those HR people standing on the side-lines looking ever-so very important. And some, dazed and confused.

It truly is an HR person's Nirvana. Clipboard heaven. Clipboard delight.

They can become damp and sweaty just thinking about it. In fact, if one of the most beautiful woman/men* in the world was to walk past this HR man/woman* (*delete as appropriate) completely naked, they would not stand a cat's chance in hell of competing with the personal ongoing development-associated clipboard.

Now I'm going to linger on the personal development aspect for just a little longer, while the objective is fresh in your minds.

Yes, personal development. Sometimes called going on-line and undertaking an Alison course. In your own time and even sometimes at your own expense. Like learning to play *'Happy Birthday'* on the penny-whistle in the style of Richard Wagner.

Now, as any fool knows, unplanned employee development is a total waste of both time and money, the only ones benefiting being the consultants who are drafted in by the HR people (whether nepotistic or otherwise) and paid an absolute and unnecessary fortune for the wonderful stuff they come up with. We all are fully aware it's generally a rehash of other people's wonderful stuff, and the HR people know we know - but hey, this is, after all, the wide and wonderful wacky world of HR.

Perhaps the greatest cop-out of all for personal ongoing development is the *'One-to-One'*. This is the Pulp Fiction of the HR world. A Quentin Tarantino epic. 50 Shades of intolerable mindless bull. The *'I will find you and I will kill you'* of HR. The co-operative method of turning both a manager and their workers into zombies.

Now I appreciate my abhorrence of HR means I tend to dismiss the majority of its workings at the drop of a hat. However, with nearly all of these workings, I don't believe I'm being too unjustifiably harsh. With the One-to-One process, I know for a fact I am not being so.

If ever there was a process that is shambolic and a total waste of time - aside from the TUPE process - this is it. Big time. It seems to have been specifically designed once completed - or if you are very lucky, discussed with you - to sit, in the case of the paper-based version, rotting away in a drawer, or for the electronic version, rotting away on someone's computer hard drive, never to again see the light of day.

For a start, the process is often undertaken by a line-manager who will have undertaken a similar and equally facile exercise with their own equally inept - that is, with regards to development - line-manager.

This person will in turn have no more than a cursory clue about the process, mainly due to a lack of knowledge, or more to the point, a lack of training and often even a straightforward lack of interest. Which at times in understandable. It is as mind-numbing as it is embarrassing for all parties involved in the process.
'Where do you see yourself in five years' time?'
'What's one thing that should change to make you happier at work?'
'What, if anything, feels harder than it should be in your day-to-day work?'
'What has been the work highlight/lowlight from the past week?'
'What else can I be doing to help progress your career?'

And so on, dribble, dribble. Drivel, drivel.

This lack of training will have resulted from the HR department not wishing to in any way divulge what they actually get up to on a day-to-day basis in this regard, that is, nothing.

The last thing the HR department want to be common knowledge amongst the workers is that they all fiddle while Rome burns. And you can bet your bottom dollar that their particular form of fiddling is all completely out of tune.

There will be great chats and copious note-taking. Wonderful sincere eyebrow shaping. Pulling of nasal hairs. Insertion of ball pens into ears. And a shedload of facile questions.

And any details requiring input on the form by the employee will have either been copied and pasted from a previous One-to-One form, or from a fellow employee, or even made up by a third (external) party who is good at creative writing.

The entire process is an unbelievable and total sham, even to the extent that is simply an insult to the employee's intelligence.

And the biggest crime is that someone in HR is earning a salary on the backs of the company's business-generating people to come up with this infantile, time-wasting guff.

Now HR is there to serve the business. Not you. They just get in the way as far as the workers are concerned.

They exist for the best interests of the employer, end of, and that is what will always win. Except in very large corporations where the very senior management, spending as they do, most of their waking day on the golf course or driving (maybe even being driven) to some vital meeting or other, are totally divorced from both their workers and reality.

Aside from generally knowing plenty of nothing, HR will always know things you don't, or will know something they can't tell you. It's the nature of the beast, and when all is said and done, there has to be some delegation of need-to-know information in an efficiently running business.

And HR will not always be confidential. Not many people realise this. If you have had a conversation with a HR person and they feel it is something that they in turn themselves feel – subjective though it might be – needs to be shared with seniors in the business in order, to perhaps prevent a *'happening'*, they will share it. Make no bones about it.

But in their defence, in some cases they may actually be obliged by law to report something. If they find out, for example, you are a serial bank robber.

So beware. Just be honest. Even if HR aren't as forthright themselves.

Chapter 7

Now, getting back on track to look as what the HR merchants actually do.

As I mentioned, for anyone on the outside, HR people seem to always look very, very busy, heads in computer spreadsheets, pushing a pen around on a very complicated-looking form, in deep, meaningful conversations on the telephone, writing vital emails (to DPD to have their cat book left in a safe place at home because they are not at home today) or dashing off to some very important meeting.

With their clipboard in tow.

Yet no one outside their own office actually knows what they do. Their spouses or partners probably don't know what they do either.

And if being truly honest, they, themselves, probably don't really know what they do. They might as well have Ben Folds in to get staff together to compose an instantaneous symphony.

People will always ask what the HR department really does and what are they paid for, mainly because, in fairness, the results of their work are not as visible as say those of a salesperson, who if they are good at what they do, help shift the company's goods and services and keep logistics, accounts, purchasing and PR busy too.

They don't seem to produce anything tangible; they aren't under the microscope for producing healthy sales figures, yet they never seem to have any time when you want to have a meeting with them.

They always seem to have an important meeting themselves that they need to rush to, and will inevitably *'pop you in their diary'* for an otherwise inconvenient time or day or ask you to *'send them an email'*.

This is because they are so frightfully important and so really, really busy. Almost so busy that they have to get someone else to breathe for them.

But really, what do they actually do?

Is it that difficult to hire someone, especially if they are blessed with being able to outsource the recruitment - at vast expense, I might add - to some recruitment agency?

In fairness to the HR bods, the one reason you can't really see what HR people do is because they have so many things to do that really are outside personnel, they have no time to report to people on what they do!

It's the equivalent of a three-ring circus that's based in three separate big tops.

And inevitably, the three big tops are located in different towns.

As I mentioned earlier, many are simply glorified administrators, given a fancy title and paid at an executive rate rather than an administrator's rate or what the actual business workers are paid! Something that understandably gets up the noses of the lesser-paid and possibly very much more efficient administrators or secretaries in the business!

A gentleman called Peter Hall writing on www.hr-faq.com on 29 December 2012 said:

'HR are simply not qualified or capable of doing a fraction of the above-mentioned tasks; most would be done by 'real professionals' in each discipline.

'HR departments are staffed by imbeciles with limited knowledge of any subject.

'When they get taken to task by someone who knows what they're talking about, they close shop and start to bully the subject.

'Most companies would be better outsourcing HR functions to companies that actually do it properly, and have staff who are up to date with employee legislation and practice, instead of having in house staff that a competent school kid could run rings round.'

The above having been said, the outsourced people would more than likely belong to a school of sharks anyway.

Because anything outsourced will take inversely and proportionally longer to do in relation to the fee being paid.

And so to the great tool absolutely loved by HR people - yes, none other than the hyperbolic and quite nonsensical psychometric test I have already referred to several times.

Wikipedia defines Psychometrics as:

'The field of study concerned with the theory and technique of psychological measurement, which includes the measurement of knowledge, abilities, attitudes, personality traits, and educational measurement. The field is primarily concerned with the construction and validation of measurement instruments such as questionnaires, tests, and personality assessments.'

In English, this translates as *'utter bull'*, devised specifically to give HR people a break from all their staff recruitment duties and allow them to wander off and nurse their vitally important clipboard or Facebook-connected smartphone over a cup of tea.

This, while the poor sap applying for the job sits in a dark, windowless room, and fills in this form-full of complete and utter mechanised tripe.

Psychometrics has everybody fooled. It's the type of thing that an innocent child would turn around and ask his father, *'Daddy, why are you making me do this rubbish?'*

In fact, it's the type of thing that a less-than-innocent 21-year-old graduate would turn around and ask his father, *'Daddy, why are you making me do this rubbish? When I could be productively on Twitter or TikTok instead.'*

Maybe it's because it's a big word that looks important. Psycho-metrics…… *'the lunatic taking measurements in the asylum'*. (Psycho-imperials perhaps, for those still using feet and inches!)

Or maybe because it's printed on a form containing absolutely tens upon tens of meaningless multiple-choice questions that help hapless HR people decide that, despite your first-class degree in engineering, you are in fact fit only for the post-room. Or failing that, perhaps you need sectioning under some obscure government Act of Parliament.

All this is decided by which particular box you shade in … with a pencil of course so the computer software can read it. Plainly the people who have invented these god-awful tests don't trust you with using a pen or ball-point.

Or trust the HR department with marking it up themselves. They don't trust you because they know when you have completed it, all you will really want to do is plunge said writing instrument into the front of the HR person's computer.

And all the time, written large over the paper *is 'there is no right or wrong answer, so be honest'*. Yes, there is no right or wrong answer because the infantile creators of this utter nonsense don't know the answers themselves! It's like asking a Jihadist *'Do you see yourself as 1) a terrorist, 2) a psychopath, 3) in dire need of lengthy incarceration?'*

Those who have completed a psychometric *'evaluation'* will appreciate where I am coming from with this. These absurd aberrations tend just to be glorified memory tests, where those with a good memory will score the highest simply because they will remember that question 11 on page two required the opposite answer to question 63 on page 11.

The former is almost without exception something not even remotely connected with work, such as *'do you like snooker?'*, while the latter being, *'do you not like snooker?'*. The idea here is that by answering *'yes'* and *'no'* respectively, you will prove that you are consistent and truthful, while at the same time potentially revealing whether you like snooker or not. Because HR people must have quite a lot of time for snooker.

And if you don't like snooker yourself, you won't fit in.

Although these tests and vintage snooker equipment do have one thing in common - both contain a load of old balls.

With most of the questions, if you answer honestly, you will score well, regardless of whether you are a brain surgeon, a shop assistant, a bank robber or even a psychopath. However, many of the questions, despite the instructions always stating, as I have mentioned, that *'there are no right or wrong answers'*, will have one rather obvious or preferred answer, and if you remember the way you answered it, you will be able to repeat it, or contradict its negative, either of which is bound to perfunctorily turn up on a later page in these ridiculous quizzes.

Generally, you will be presented with statements describing various ways of feeling or acting and asked to answer each one on a 2 point, 5 point or 7-point scale.

The number of questions you are expected to answer varies from about 50 to 200, depending on the duration of the test or how much attention the HR person's clipboard needs, or for that matter, how much of an afternoon nap they might require while you complete it.

One of the popular questions is:

'I enjoy working on my own'
a) true
b) false

The cynic, of which I am one, will agree that, yes, as stated in the instructions, there is no right or wrong answer.

However, regardless of how you answer it, they have you bang to rights.

If you reply *'I enjoy working on my own'*, the inference is that you are not a *'team player'*. Yet were you to reply *'I do not enjoy working on my own'*, the inference then is that you have no initiative and like to be told what to do all the time.

So, you are snookered from the word go. Or not snookered, as the question on page 11, if you have already answered, *'I don't like snooker',* earlier on page two.

Another great favourite is:

'I enjoy parties and other social occasions.'
a) strongly disagree
b) disagree
c) neutral
d) agree
e) strongly agree

If you agree, then you might be perceived as someone who avoids Mondays like the plague. This is because you've been out all weekend partying, and by the time 6.30am Monday morning comes around, you now are in possession of the mother of all hang-overs. So, you will be rather disinclined to raise yourself out of your sleeping pit and really don't need to trundle into the office for a day's work to enjoy managers moaning *('going forward', 'thinking outside the box'* and *'ring-fencing'* all day long).

Or suffer whining customers that *'are always right'* bleating at you from nine to five, even though those self-same customers are regularly wrong.

On the other hand, if you disagree, you are perceived as being a miserable old sod who keeps to themselves, doesn't get involved, certainly won't attend any work's events, and in fact, seems to have the social skills of a daffodil.

'Work is the most important thing in my life'
a) very strongly disagree
b) strongly disagrees
c) disagree

d) neutral
e) agree
f) strongly agree
g) very strongly agree
h) pass the sick bag Alice

Again, no matter how you answer, and regardless of how much stress is put on there *'not being a right or wrong answer'*, you're well and truly beggared. Especially when, several pages further on, the same question is asked, this time, cunningly disguised as a different question.

If *'work is not the most important thing in your life'*, then you might not necessarily be deemed to be the correct person for a job where the directors expect you to slave away 12-hours a day meeting sales targets while they swan off in their executive BMW's to play golf for the week - cars, golf club membership, clubs and meals that your sweat and toil have provided. These people don't think for even one minute that not only might you have a family to go home to, but that you actually have other interests outside providing them with an obscene profit and salary, or their useless shareholders with a return.

On the other hand, if you find that *'work is the most important thing in your life'*, you might be perceived as not only being rather sad, with no outside interests, but as someone who is a threat to those who are somewhat more work-shy than yourself, and consequently an even bigger threat to their more laid-back approach to work.

I'm afraid, therefore, you are shafted no matter which *'there is no correct or incorrect'* answer you decide upon.

Deep joy!

Some of the questions are downright insulting, and even the most logical of thinkers would have trouble with them. The type I refer to are the ones where you are presented with several alternative answers where none are appropriate. These are meant to reach deep into your inner psyche to see how you think.

For example, the question might be something along the lines of:

'If you were to knock someone down with your motor car, would you prefer that it was':

a) a pensioner
b) a student
c) a child
d) a housewife
e) a reality star.

Typically, the option f) *'swerve to avoid'* is not offered, but in the eyes of those on day-release from a restraining order who invented this total waste of time and effort, the option a*), a pensioner*, would score the best on the basis of the pensioner having enjoyed a good innings so is potentially more deserving of being knocked down, while the remainder of the people in the option have the rest of their lives ahead of them.

Yes, OK, I'm being rather silly again, but you do know what I mean. HR is sometimes so silly, so why shouldn't I be?

Yet how you fare in these mindless quizzes is decided either by comparing your set of answers to an arbitrarily set of base figures provided by the salespeople who sold the HR bozos the quiz in the first place, or by feeding the results into a computer and allowing it to allocate marks via the shaded-in box system that reads from the stored master-card.

Account is not taken, for example, that the question might be completely at odds with reality; that no one in their right mind would wish to choose to have a motor-car accident.

Neither is in factored in that if it's a minor bump, the student possibly has the best chance of making a full and swift recovery, whereas an equivalent bump to the pensioner could see them in hospital for several weeks with a broken bone, at vast discomfort to themselves and at vast expense to the emergency and health services.

Needless to say, I do recognise that personality is of great importance in success at work, but I feel there is nothing like a professionally-run interview to take stock of this. And these tests are as unreal as the scenarios they present the candidate with.

We have all had occasions where we have telephoned someone who sounds like a house-brick on medication and where getting an appropriate response to a question we pose is the equivalent of getting an answer to a direct yes-or-no question from a politician on the BBC's *'Question Time'*.

Or perhaps you may remember meeting someone with a wet handshake who has the personality of an out-of-date lettuce and leaves (lettuce and leaves – oh how poetic) you shuddering to the core. Unless, of course, you are recruiting for a Stephen King horror movie.

The principle behind these tests is that they think it's possible to quantify a person's personality by asking irrelevant questions about their feelings, thoughts and behaviour in a variety of situations both at work and outside of work. But they are totally unreal, and, as I have mentioned, they don't take into account the individual's ability to memorise previous questions, or the fact that someone might be quite logical in thought, seem very sensible, but whose leisure hobby is stealing cars or robbing post offices.

Personally, I believe the HR people simply take these questions back and have a good laugh together over one of the many tea breaks they need to take during the day in order to equalise their own work-life imbalances.

If we take a trip back to 2008, there was a survey on employee engagement by Ceridian, who said at the time they were one of the largest providers of human resource services in the world. No mean feat in itself to be the largest in the world, although I'd never heard of them. So, I'll therefore take their word for it.

This survey revealed that half of office workers felt HR teams make no difference to their jobs, while nearly a quarter, at 22 per cent, actually consider the HR function in their workplace makes them less than satisfied by getting things wrong.

This bodes extremely well for the industry, as you will no doubt agree.

It appears from that particular survey that male office workers, some 26 per cent, were more likely to feel dissatisfaction with the function. However, younger (and less world-wise/more-naive) employees aged 16 to 24 were more positive about the function's contribution, with 19 per cent declaring they could see some benefit from the HR initiatives introduced into their workplace.

Doug Sawers, managing director of Ceridian in the UK, commented:

With only four per cent of respondents lacking an HR department, this makes grim reading for the HR function.

Just three per cent of employees surveyed considered the function as important as their manager, which reinforces the view that HR should make sure they get the basics right and provide line managers with the necessary tools to deliver effective people management.

HR can then concentrate on innovating in critical areas such as employee acquisition, retention and performance to allow the function to deliver business-led strategic initiatives, which keep their organisations ahead of the competition.'

Some of the other findings from the survey concluded:

45 per cent did not think their employer understood how well they were managed

older workers, aged over 45, were more than twice as likely to look for a new job in the next year because they had a really poor manager

just under a third thought they suffered from inadequate training

younger employees aged 16 to 24 were more positive than the rest of the workforce on the helpfulness of performance reviews and of the quality of training provided

being better recognised and thanked for their contribution was the third most influential factor in moving to a new employer.

Interesting reading.

The sample was taken from just under 1,100 respondents.

Chapter 8

So aside from the obvious answer, why, really, do we hate HR so much, to the extent that it is top of the stack, hate-wise that is?

There does have to be something intrinsically wrong that we all loathe HR to the levels we do, and it's not alone for simply being the equivalent of the Four Men of the Apocalypse when it comes to hiring and firing capability within an organisation.

Why do they seem, in the eyes of so many to, if not actually do, such a bad job, and is there any way of fixing the problem, or fixing the fact that they all appear to do such a bad job?

While it's Ok for me to sit here at my keyboard and vent my spleen at what I (and many others) justifiably consider to be a completely idiotic business function, I fully concede that it is only fair and equitable that I support this venting with something a little more constructive!

My own justification is a combination of what I have seen over the years coupled with my own experience of being on the receiving end of one of the most amateurish and dishonest excuse for a TUPE process I have ever witnessed.

I already mentioned that The Transfer of Undertakings (Protection of Employment) Regulations 2006 is better known in its colloquial form as TUPE, pronounced 'tu-pee', and for those who have had the misfortune to be part of one, the accent is very much on the 'pee', as a complete urine-take it indeed is.

And not worth much more than 2p. This is the UK's implementation of the European Union Business Transfers Directive.

It is an important part of UK labour law, meant to offer protection to employees whose job of work is being transferred to another business.

The 2006 regulations replaced the old 1981 regulations which implemented the original Directive.

This particular disgraceful sham was lorded over by a very distasteful individual who was without doubt paid a small fortune (by their pal the CEO) to inflict total misery on we mushrooms who were constantly kept in the dark and fed continual and total fiction about the entire process.

A complete whitewash from start to finish.

At the same time, incredible fiction was dreamt up so the company could attempt to completely abrogate its responsibilities at the lowest possible cost.

They only ever had the intention of TUPEing just a mere handful of favourite people (the ones who could lick backsides the most efficiently) from one part of the business to the other, while they had all staff in at their shambolic *'consultative'* meetings during the *'process'*. Yes, it's slightly complicated, but not too difficult to grasp the situation.

In essence, the managing Organisation A was receiving funding from Organisation B to manage and run Organisation C.

I was under contract to Organisation C to provide my area of expertise to not only Organisation C but also at the same time provide my services to managing Organisation A and with its own various activities.

I hope you can picture the situation.

Now, the funding from Organisation B to the managing Organisation A for running Organisation C was ending.

This meant that instead of simply being upfront and personal and organising meaningful redundancy discussions, a ridiculous TUPE was instituted, headed by the distasteful individual I mentioned.

There wasn't really a pure takeover in the true sense of the word, particularly as I had been doing work for both the third-party subsidised Organisation C and the managing Organisation A.

And it is also a huge coincidence (not) that after I had been made redundant by this totally dishonest process under a ridiculous and 100% dishonest shafting process (having taken legal action I had walked away with a £5,500 gagging payoff), a few months later, the former (and redundant) manager from the now defunct Organisation B was suddenly in place doing my job (thus explaining the gagging order).

It was utterly and without any doubt whatsoever, blatant constructive dismissal for me, but, because of my short tenure before the funded Organisation C was defunded and shut down, Employment Law could not come to the rescue, despite the fact that a very senior employment counsel (who I couldn't at the time afford to represent me) told me I had been 100% shafted, in his eyes the gagging order being enough proof on its own.

The shady and nasty side of HR that these types can get away with is simply as abhorrent as it is shameful.

Nevertheless, I feel it is only fair to those honest and professional personnel practitioners out there that I delve a little deeper to justify both my vitriol and my deeply embedded mistrust of HR and all it stands for.

We live in a world where knowledge - and ability to get the job done or the sales confirmed - is power. And discovering and encouraging the talent to attain this should be one of the most important jobs in an organisation. So, is there any particular reason that HR, personnel or the staffing function - whatever you choose to call it - is carried out so badly?

How can it be fixed?

Is there an easy answer?

I extract from an excellent article some time back by a gentleman called Keith H. Hammonds, who was the deputy editor of Fast Company Magazine in New York.

He's a graduate of Harvard Business School, so certainly has a reasonable idea of what he is talking about. I have italicised this lengthy edited extract, as I don't wish to claim it in any way as my own, but have used it because, in my opinion, it is so good. The non-italic text is my own commentary, as he hits upon almost everything I have myself found over the years.

Keith began by recounting his visit to a two-day *'strategic HR leadership,'* conference in Las Vegas. His introduction was as follows:

'Well, here's a rockin' party: a gathering of several hundred, mid-level, human resource executives in Las Vegas. They are here, ensconced for two days at faux-glam Caesars Palace, to confer on 'strategic HR leadership,' a conceit that sounds, to the lay observer, at once frightening and self-contradictory. If not plain laughable.

'Because let's face it: After close to 20 years of hopeful rhetoric about becoming 'strategic partners' with a 'seat at the table' where the business decisions that matter are made, most human-resources professionals aren't nearly there. They have no seat, and the table is locked inside a conference room to which they have no key. HR people are, for most practical purposes, neither strategic nor leaders.

'The human-resources trade long ago proved itself, at best, a necessary evil -- and at worst, a dark bureaucratic force that blindly enforces nonsensical rules, resists creativity, and impedes constructive change. HR is the corporate function with the greatest potential -- the key driver, in theory, of business performance -- and also the one that most consistently under-delivers. And I am here to find out why.

'Why are annual performance appraisals so time-consuming -- and so routinely useless?'

Now this is indeed an interesting point that Keith raises. Because despite the alleged *'advances'* in HR, annual performance appraisals do indeed remain a time-consuming waste of peoples' effort and, er, time.

Presenting, as they invariably do, often unintelligible and unreal questions, completed unrelated to a person's job function, all written down on several sheets of paper (the number of sheets of questions being inversely proportional to the intelligence of the HR department and/or the number of clipboards they own) that are filed and never referred to again until the next appraisal, often by a completely different person and one who in reality hasn't a clue what you do in your job.

Or what they do in theirs for that matter.

These appraisal forms are becoming so facile and off-topic, in many instances asking irrelevant questions whose heading - but not body content copy - is simply changed from one year's quarter assignation to the following quarter.

For example, asking someone who is quite happy as a fully trained and qualified fork-lift operator what their *'aspirations'* for the following year are, or where they *'see themselves this time next year'* is actually an insult to their intelligence. A happy, fully trained and qualified fork-lift operator does not suddenly have the aspiration to become the company accountant or marketing director *'this time next year'*.

The primary *'aspirations'* nowadays is that they would like the assurance that they can *'see themselves this time next year'* having a job. Perhaps the HR people might be able to better employ themselves asking mayflies *'where they see themselves at the end of the day'*, because in that way, they can get leverage extra bits of unnecessary jargon into their daily conversation.

Also fast becoming the norm for ordinary working people asked to complete these effronteries to their hard work and devotion to the company, is the common practice of someone else completing the form for them, rendering the appraisal form rather redundant even before it leaves the PC.

Normal working people, who can't really be bothered with this witless practice, preferring as they generally do just to get on with their jobs, are now, out of sheer frustration at being asked to fill in something they find so useless as to border on the offensive. If you are a refuse collector, you get through your rounds on time, you like and are in turn likes by your colleagues, and your customers – the residents – appreciate your efforts, do you really need to complete a boat-rocking exercise?

Many people going thought these appraisals often ask their spouses or early adult children to complete any advance paper work in connection with it.

For them it has become the farcical, annual norm.

And what is most sad of all is that the HR department who take the whole process so seriously and hang on every word written in the appraisal by the employee (not!), don't even notice this prior to filing it in their perpetual folder, shredder, or wherever they file it never to be seen or referred to again in.

Keith asks:

'Why is HR so often a henchman for the chief financial officer, finding ever-more ingenious ways to cut benefits and hack at payroll? Why do its communications - when we can understand them at all - so often flout reality?

Why are so many people-processes duplicative and wasteful, creating a forest of paperwork for every minor transaction? And why does HR insist on sameness as a proxy for equity?'

Again, he's not wrong! If there's one thing that HR generates besides high blood pressure and heartache for workers, it's a paper mountain.

With a summit that will never be reached.

They are great at disguising their lack of contribution to a business through a mound of paper.

'It's no wonder that we hate HR. In a 2005 survey by consultancy Hays Group, just 40% of employees commended their companies for retaining high-quality workers. Just 41% agreed that performance evaluations were fair. Only 58% rated their job training as favourable. Most said they had few opportunities for advancement - and that they didn't know, in any case, what was required to move up. Most telling, only about half of workers below the manager level believed their companies took a genuine interest in their well-being.'

Again, all true. Employees can fill in appraisal forms and ridiculous *'where do you see yourself this time next year'* (I see myself living in the Maldives if I win the lottery in the intervening 12 months) boxes until they are blue in the face, but if the line manager (often totally untrained in any form of appraisal work) can't be bothered, or the employee's face doesn't fit, then it's a totally wasteful exercise.

This is even more so when the employee is actually better at their job than the line manager, so they are seen as a threat and purposefully ignored by them (the line manager). All too often the appraisal is about as objective as it is objectionable, only less so! In a three-tier structure of workers, middle management and senior management, middle management is equally the curse of the working classes.

And it's the vital working classes in most major organisations who are overlooked. Because they have the expertise. And they are the threat to the middle management who were most probably once working classes in that very business themselves.

Despite how much I despise HR, I am loath to have to admit that most of the people engaged in it are, by and large, thoroughly decent enough human beings. It's just what they do is a waste of space, time and effort. Really more to be pitied than laughed at.

Because it's not really their fault. They were, like any youngster deciding on their career and university path, somewhat impressionable, and in their defence, they wouldn't have realised that the profession they were heading towards would be the very one most derided by *'the workers'*. Because no one told them, because if they did, there would be plenty of unemployed university lecturers.

Keith continues:

'But then the facade cracks. It happens at an afternoon presentation called 'From Technicians to Consultants: How to Transform Your HR Staff into Strategic Business Partners.' The speaker, Julie Muckler, is senior vice president of human resources at Wells Fargo Home Mortgage. She is an enthusiastic woman with a broad smile and 20 years of experience at companies such as Johnson & Johnson and General Tire. She has degrees in consumer economics and human resources and organizational development.

And I have no idea what she's talking about.'

Yes, I can see where Keith is coming from. If you can't dazzle them with brilliance, then baffle them with bull. And keep smiling, as it makes people wonder what you are up to!

'There is mention of 'internal action learning' and 'being more planful in my approach, leveraging internal resources and involving external resources - and she leaves her audience dazed. That evening, even the human-resources pros confide they didn't understand much of it, either.

'This, friends, is the trouble with HR. We all know that. Human resources execs should be making the most of our, well, human resources -- finding the best hires, nurturing the stars, fostering a productive work environment -- just as IT runs the computers and finance minds the capital. HR should be joined to business strategy at the hip.

So, in a nutshell, Keith is confirming very much what I have already said - HR seems to be very much run as a *'clipboard culture'*, never losing any opportunity to make something up that can be covered by either a jargon-ridden or jingoistic reference.

Keith claims that:

'HR people aren't the sharpest tacks in the box'.

He further says that:

'Any ambitious young thing newly graduated from a top college or B-school with your eye on a rewarding career in business will not to join the human-resources dance as their first option.' And a management professor at one leading school said: 'The best and the brightest don't go into HR.'

Now Keith admits that while intelligent people sometimes enter HR, none are really business people.

They are simply not equipped for it, regardless of how good their HR degree might be.

Do they really, for example, know who the business's customers are? Would they recognise or even fall over a customer if they saw them in the reception area? Do they know what makes the customer a customer and the reason they actually buy products or services from the company?

Of course, they don't. They've come straight from some university course where they've never even seen a real business working before, let alone worked on a shop floor or in a customer-facing environment.

And if there a defensive reason for their purchase relating to the customer's own business, how does that relationship work?

Do they know about that? No, probably not. To the HR person, the customer is nothing other than a seven-letter word. Because if their recruitment advertisements are anything to go by, they certainly can't spell.

If you'd like to read Keith's full article, it's here https://www.ou.edu/russell/4153/Hammond.pdf or shorturl.at/eoJ39

Chapter 9

So, the million-dollar question comes back to, does HR actually know who the business competition in the business they work for is, or are?

No, according to many observers and much research, they appear not to. And they certainly won't know what the competition does, either well, or badly. And there's not a hope in a puff of smoke's chance that the HR people would know how things fare regarding the relationship between the business, the customer and the competition.

But in fairness, as HR are not in the business of sales or purchasing, why should any but the most proactive HR executive care about those comparatives if they lie outside their knowledge areas and there might be no incentive in the company culture for them to find out. To cut HR a bit of slack, would it be reasonable to expect the marketing executive at the company to know all about the accountancy software the company accountant uses?

Either way, it would appear that HR can't cope with the concepts of efficiency and value at the same time. They are great at activities and activity generation, but totally lacking in actually delivering anything of value or worth. Because again, for a bit of balance, they have not been taught. The only thing they know is HR. It's the employment equivalent of NIMBYism – Not In My Back Yard, or NIMO, Not In My Office.

However, in order to add an element of balance, I should say that not all are this way inclined. It's just the nature of the beast.

It would appear that the HR seems to want to invest in activities – happy-clap days out team building, ignoring that the team will often retire to the pub together at the end of the week, or in more closely-knit organisations, socialise together anyway. They don't need someone with a clipboard taking them away for the day to undertake irrelevant activities together.

They seem to forget - if indeed they were aware in the first place - that the outcome of any activity is the important factor for the business, not how well the staff can put on an impromptu pantomime in some luxurious hotel, enjoyable though a day away from the office, phones and those annoying people called customers might be.

The impromptu pantomime might to a degree help – with a very small '*h*' - employees and managers, but it doesn't help customers, shareholders or investors. It doesn't shift product, and sell services.

The same could be said for the basic recruitment process.

Yes. Recruitment. That's the process personnel used to manage for years quite well before it transformed into HR and all the associated flannel that was lumped on personnel when it subsequently went academic, institutional and metamorphosed into HR.

The arrival of HR marked the tipping point when personnel stopped its basic recruitment function and became somewhat of an internal outsourcing agency for company staff.

(Again, to try and be somewhat objective, this hasn't happened with all organisations).

HR began producing job specifications for positions, and feeding them out to recruitment consultants to do all the donkey work in their own, inimitable and commission-laden way. The arguments for this are many and several, some positive, but many are negative.

The main negative one is that the line manager for the position knows exactly who and what they require. On the other hand, the recruitment consultant, unless fully conversant and with practical experience of the particular post in question, tends to know absolutely nothing. And if they are simply *"my leading client"* and purely commission-orientated, the chances are they only have an extremely basic understanding of the business they are recruiting for.

What this means is that a very suitable candidate for the job could be easily overlooked because they don't *'tick the boxes'* that the consultant thinks are those boxes that need ticking.

A small engineering firm outsourcing its recruitment to a specialist engineering recruitment firm could very well, providing the consultant is very well versed in the position from practical experience, find a suitable candidate.

However, a large generalist consultancy, recruiting in a text book and broad-spectrum manner, is simply not equipped to recruit a specialist for any industry, irrespective of how well they talk the talk.

And if the recruitment consultant takes an aversion to the recruit for a reason not connected with the actual position (they don't like their hair), it in essence becomes an unfair process from the outset.

And recruitment consultants are increasingly resorting to automatic CV scanning software to assess potential candidates. For some specialist trades, where perhaps the candidate is better at their job than they are at preparing a CV might, therefore, not receive the opportunity of an interview because the machine hasn't picked up the pertinent information that the candidate may have mistakenly left out.

While an applicant should have some basic form of experiential communication and writing ability, they shouldn't just have to rely on a clinical CV in order to be considered for a job interview.

Another aspect is one of HR gap-filling as opposed to recruitment. A vacant position in a company is under the management of a less-than-popular manager, so understandably, no internal candidates comes forward, despite several being suitably qualified for the position.

So, here's a scenario:

A talented young marketing executive, straight out of business school, accepts a job offer with a major corporation. She interviews for openings in several departments in the organisation, only to be told by HR that only one department is interested in her. But she learns later they all had been interested and indeed impressed. She had been railroaded into the job, under the supervision of a widely reviled manager, because no one inside the company would take it.

So, did HR do its job?

On the one hand, it undertook the main function, that is, it filled the position. It did what it had to do. Having someone in place who would meekly accept it and get on with it made corporate sense. But the marketing executive was livid. And very unhappy. So, the recruitment was doomed from the outset.

So, after a few months, she most probably will have left. All the costs of recruitment up in smoke with the ramifications of further costs in replacing her.

Part of the problem here with a large organisation is that there is a good chance the real cost of its HR department's action would never show up on its financial or performance records. HR can always (well nearly always – I don't want to in anyway encourage big heads in HR) show the number of employees it has on the books, will have a drawer full of wonderful, never-to-be-referred-to-again *'performance evaluations'*, and should know how satisfied employees are with the state of things in the organisation.

But it will be quite unlikely to have linked the way it (HR) performs to the actual performance of the business.

Whether this is just because it is acknowledged that HR doesn't actually contribute anything to the profitability of the business (in fairness, it is not really in a position of being able do so), and is in fact just simply a burden on the business (which it is), is the 64-million-dollar question.

You might end up agreeing with this cynic that HR perhaps doesn't work.

If this is indeed the case, why is it still around, and why do HR departments breed at every opportune moment?

Some people have gone further than my experience-based loathing to suggest that one of the reasons HR put staff through the idiotic performance appraisal every year is because this is the most valuable function they can actually provide for an organisation. They do it to simply protect themselves from their own employees.

Garold L. Markle, who was a long-time human resource executive at Exxon and Shell Offshore and who now runs his own business once said:

'They (companies and/or organisations) put a piece of paper between you and employees, so if you ever have a confrontation, you can go to the file and say, 'Here, I've documented this problem.'

Of course, to every action there is an opposite reaction, and while HR can at times be by and large totally useless, there are people there who aren't altogether stupid, despite giving a pretty good impression of being so.

They go on the defensive, because over the past three decades or so there has been an incredible raft of legislation, regulation and rules introduced to allegedly protect the worker (but bear in mind the farcical and by-and-large dishonest TUPE I referred to earlier – designed to protect the worker but not even getting as near as the next city!).

This legislation with accompanying regulation and rules – be it Health and Safety, Age Discrimination, Equal Opportunity, Maternity and the rest, really are a complete minefield, and companies now have to be extremely careful.

HR people now have to be very careful too. Because it's the one area where they can actually have impact. And not all of it positive. And given the American litigation culture that is slowly seeping wholesale into British society, encouraging people to sue over the slightest thing, who can blame them.

However, playing the gatekeeper on this doesn't help with the overall perception of HR as anything but the dysfunctional and at times non-essential I have mentioned it is thus far! Making sure an organisation doesn't break the rules could be the job of a top flight legal administrator instead.

Therefore, one of the single biggest problems continues to be that HR people are all rather standard in what they do, despite the complexity and diversity of an organisation or business and its workforce. They take the easy option of trying to be, at all times, a one size that fits all.

But it invariably doesn't, hence HR continually returns the big failure, as far as employees perceive it.

They're incredible at comparing sector salaries on a job-by-job basis so they can recommend, if any, salary increases. In hard times they can send a job appraisal back to a manager if they feel said manager is rating the employee too highly and it could end up with a disproportionate pay increase that, heaven help everyone, could be higher than the company average!

And by so doing, they essentially are experts at short-termism, and completely useless at, amongst their many failings, long-term things.

HR really has to face up to it. It needs to stop shuffling bits of paper, waving clipboards, outsourcing its own responsibilities to recruitment agency sharks, organising happy-clappy bonding sessions and doling out useless and never-referred-to-again appraisals.

It now needs to step up to the plate and actually start doing something useful. Become more company-centric and strategic. Stop being so sincere when they don't really mean at all that *'employees are the company's most important asset'.*

So bl**dy well prove it to us all then!

Because despite what I have said and how much I loathe everything HR stands for, it can be done correctly, and more importantly, done ethically.

Even in organisations that have the most ineffectual and dysfunctional HR department on earth.

As many seemingly compete to try and have.

There are, as I have found over the years, some good, honest, caring, professional HR people out there among the detritus of HR bumblers, evil and dishonest TUPE'ers and Health and Safety executives who are nothing but a jobsworth danger to all employees around them.

There seems, sadly, to be a pattern of those who are not necessarily being specifically HR-trained making the best HR professionals.

The ones who move over to HR from other areas, thus bringing a host of business and life skills, appear to be altogether much better than those who arrive fresh from university, knock a couple of nails into the wall from which to hang their wonderful degree and CIPD membership certificates, and then get their clipboard out and start to impressively and importantly shuffle papers around their desk.

Now I appreciate that with any work sector, one needs to gain experience to prove one's worth, but unfortunately, HR seems to be one sector where practitioners are let loose with gay abandon irrespective of their level of knowledge, or more importantly, their level of capability. And this results in their worth being nigh on impossible to value. Because sadly, in the world of HR, knowledge and capability tend to be on different planets. And not necessarily in the same universe.

However, it would be unfair of me not to mention that is can be quite hard to align an HR strategy to a business strategy, because things in business can change so quickly. For example, a dramatic and rather quick shift in buying habits (for example that caused by the recent imposition of these false retail-orientated days such as Black Friday, Sales Thursday, Bloody Sunday and all the other fakery days are much easier for business to respond, or even react (subtle difference) to.

HR, however, certainly from a legislation point of view, can't, in the case of for example something related to disability, roll an initiative out overnight. It just can't be done.

Another problem faced by HR is outsourcing, or in English, paying someone not employed by the company to do something for the company. Mention outsourcing, and immediately there's an uncomfortable shifting on the chair from one bottom cheek to the other.

However, it's been going on for almost as long as business itself has. If you need a brochure, you usually ask a printing house. If you need a logo, you usually ask a graphic designer. And most small companies will employ the services of an accountant or solicitor when they need one.

And when it comes to outsourcing, HR is an altogether different kettle of fish. Purists will say the idea is that it's just the little HR things that get outsourced, thus leaving the in-house professionals to get on with the bigger things.

Unfortunately, it's only the little things that HR tend to be any good at. The clipboard things. The hand delivery of pay slips in envelopes things. The management of jumping up and down on coloured squares of paper in a hotel for team building things. HR are no good at the big things. Well, not so much no good at, but more so, incapable of. And if it is such a vital function of a business, this certainly shouldn't be the case.

And naturally enough, when it comes to employment and the hiring of staff, the recruitment sharks will seize upon this big time.

A small story.

Two gentlemen undertook a quite interesting experiment some time back. Bradley Ruffle at Ben-Gurion University and Ze'ev Shtudiner at Ariel University Centre were trying to answer the question as to whether being good looking could help you find a job.

Surprisingly, they found that if you are a good-looking lady, you will find it quite difficult to secure that job! It seems that 93 percent of the HR staff who make the final call whether to call someone in for an interview are female. HR women are eager to meet their ideal man and apparently are jealous of beautiful women. So, a business could be losing out big style on talented people and subsequently wasting time with unsuitable ones based purely on their looks and the whim of the useless HR staff.

Now, back to the CIPD – the Chartered Institute of Personnel and Development. Luckily the 'C' in 'CIPD' doesn't stand for certified.

In late 2007, they stopped postings on their website from anyone who was complaining about the organisation. There also seemed to also be shatter of concerns about its Disability Discrimination Act (DDA) compliance. At least that was the case according to Juliet LeFevre, writing on the HRZone website way back on 01 October 2007.

In late 2010 it was reported that the then chief executive officer of the organisation, according to their accounts, had received an unbelievably eye-watering £400,000 salary with an £85,000 bonus - up 49% from the previously and plainly meagre bonus of £57,000 the previous year – the bonus representing a sum many of the CIPD's membership would most certainly be happy with as a salary alone.

And do remember, the Prime Minister of the UK has to manage on a mere £142,500 (at the time of the 1st edition of this book – it is now £161,401), and the President of the United States on a mere approximate £276,000 (at the time of the 1st edition of this book – it is now £320,000).

This particular CEO was being cited as the Fred Goodwin (for those of you who can't recall, he was the ex-Sir who was almost single-handedly responsible for the UK's early noughties banking crisis) of HR. And is it in anyway surprising when one compares the salary of the president of the most powerful nation in the western world falling over £200,000 short of what she was earning for happy-clappiness!

What was laughable and derided was that in receiving this incredible salary and unbelievable bonus, this particular CEO presided over a period where revenue for the CIPD had dropped 23.7% (excluding the acquired income from an aggressive takeover), revenue from branches down 45.6%, research down 57% (including a totally ridiculed report, later pulled after an outcry, on the spend on Quangos in Education and Skills [cynics might remark that it was perhaps a thinly-veiled attack on CIPD rivals]), magazine revenue down 83%, investment returns down 74.7% and a membership up in arms about how things are run.

Not a bad return on investment for incredibly poor performance and leadership, not to forget the bonus reward.

Ah yes. Leadership. The CIPD was at the time superb at wittering and twittering on about leadership. But as an organisation, perhaps a beacon of black light for fiscal failure and total lack of leadership? A salary of £400,000 and bonus increased to £85,000. Almost Half a million pounds as a reward for abject failure. Inversely proportional to the performance and achievement. £856 a day take home pay. £18,500 a month after tax.

This is almost on a par with the consultants and legal people who have been ripping off UK plc at a national level for years.

Nice work if you can avoid it! And a very strange position for the main professional body for HR and training to find itself in. And it doesn't end there. No. This is HR's selfless Chartered Institute of Personnel and Development. In the accounts, the CEO also had a nice little £6,000 added on top of the £400,000 salary. And something called £13,000 benefits in kind, whatever they might have been on such a huge salary. And a pension.

To remind you. That's £856-a-day take home pay. Just two weeks and you can afford a pretty reasonable brand-new car on that sort of salary. And don't forget the £85,000 bonus for underperformance and failure at the end of the year. Great little earner this HR mismanagement thing, eh? I bet you, dear reader, aren't the least bit jealous, are you.

Maybe you should retire from work altogether and go into HR!

But hold the bus. It's not over yet! Oh no! The CEO was at the same time firing on all guns creating a magnificent culture of greed with a dramatic 50% increase in the number of staff on £60,000 plus, up from 14 in 2009 to 21 in 2010.

And this was all under-achieved with a rather aggressive push into commercial activities, using an acquisition (sum paid £3.8 million plus a £900,000 earn-out) and its own brand to blow any perceptible commercial competition out of the water.

And this is a registered business charity if you don't mind!

The membership must have been really ever so pleased. But it is completely and shamefully symptomatic, or perhaps par for the course that the *'leaders'* of HR might actually be as lacklustre as the actual profession is itself.

I haven't checked what the current CEO's remuneration is. No doubt it's on their website.

But I must make mention that at the time of updating, their current CEO is named Peter Cheese.

Please don't spread that around.

I haven't checked, but I can only assume that under the *'new'* leadership things must have improved, otherwise the Institute's membership wouldn't have increased in the intervening years.

And I do fully concede that HR, like any trade, does most definitely need its professional umbrella organisation for its members, to pass on knowledge, offer networking opportunities, run conferences as well as general member get-togethers. Not to forget research into employment via its members.

However, if ever there was a profession needing Government intervention, it would appear HR is the prime suspect. After all, it deals not just with organisational recruitment matters, but with people's lives and livelihoods. So, it cannot and really ought not to go on unchecked. It cannot be the guardian of it's own activities.

Then again, and from experience I might add, it appears that business charities (and to a degree the ordinary public-facing charities, if reports in the media are anything to go by), can get away with anything, including overpaying their chief executives and senior staff while performing exceptionally badly themselves.

As for headhunting. Nothing to do with cowboys and Indians. That was scalp hunting.

Now here is totally same but different can of worms. Many people wonder what the difference is between a head-hunter and a recruitment agent is. The head-hunter will swear blind that there is a huge difference. The head-hunter will swear that he actually works for a living, and will happily accuse the recruitment consultant of being not much more than dirt on the ground claiming commission for doing nothing.

On the other hand, the recruitment consultant will swear the head-hunter is aptly named because he commits as near as makes no difference to recruitment murder. For a huge fee. Actually, nearly always a massive fee.

Remember folks, both are associated with HR, so do take what each says with a very small pinch of salt. Because what each has in common with the other is, each is a shark. Swimming merrily in ineffectual, HR-infested waters, wreaking havoc on innocent job-swimmers wherever they go.

Were you to give a head-hunter and recruitment consultant a baseball bat each and lock them in a room together, half an hour later you'd find two dead bodies, each with a notice pinned on claiming *'I'm more dead than he is'*. Or knowing recruitment, the notice would read *'I'm the leading dead person in here'*.

The head-hunter will accuse the recruiter of not being a true head-hunter. The recruiter will accuse the head-hunter of not knowing their client thoroughly.

The head-hunter will claim he searches the *'whole of the market'* and finds *'better'* people. The recruiter will say the head-hunter doesn't, because he, the recruiter, does.

The head-hunter will say the recruiter is just in a *'CV race with other agencies'*. The recruiter will say the head-hunter has a very weak database so wouldn't be able to enter a CV race anyway.

Both will claim to put in shed-loads of time and always identify the best possible person for the job. And, of course, as I mentioned earlier, both will claim they are working for *'my client'* who inevitably is *'a leader in their field'*. Which is OK if you're an unemployed farmer. Always the best in their field.

Just like a tractor leads a plough. Or a carrot leads an ass.

As they say in the upper echelons of UK Parliament. *'Complete and utter b*llox'*.

Chapter 10

Now, on to recruitment consultants.

By and large, quite wonderful people. Sort of. In much the same way as it is better to catch a severe, debilitating cold rather than influenza.

I've already mentioned them. While some, like in any industry, can be good at what they do, others are bad, bordering on criminal. In fact, if the Department for Work and Pensions were to appoint a *'Recruitment Tsar'*, he or she would be busy on a 24-hour, seven-day stint, week-in, week-out.

Sadly, some recruitment consultants are so bad at what they do they can actually adversely affect your career should you engage with them.

Before going any further, I should mention that in-house recruiters and in-house head-hunters are the ones that tend to do what it says on their clipboards. They are actually tasked by the company they work for with finding someone, so if you are contacted by a genuine, in-house one of these, go with him or her. They have no commission-chasing axe to grind and are usually acting in the best interests of the company they work for, that is, filling an internal vacancy. And they are generally not all bad, simply just doing their job.
But do remember, if first contact is by phone or email, first impressions last and all that, so don't be silly or smart.

The big problem with external recruiters in general is the way they work. They tend to be paid in one of three ways.

Either:

1. A percentage of the final salary of the jobs they find for people
2. How many people they find if on a *'mission'* to fill places

or perhaps the most unethical of the lot,

3. The budgeted job, where they have been given a specific amount to spend. This means that they will try and maximise the amount they retain, unless the *'my client'* (who will of course be a leading company) sets a specific rate that the prospective employee or contractor is to be paid for the job with the recruiter retaining the balance.

As I mentioned earlier, you then start all your recruitment advertisement with *'My client is a leading . . . . .'* despite the fact they are not your client (you contacted them after they omitted *'no agencies'* from their most recent recruitment advertisement) and you - and they - have no proof whatsoever that they are actually *'leading'* – you just say they are to give them a big head so they will pay you for the recruitment service they really didn't need.

Although HR and recruitment has grown rather untrustworthy, attracting levels of mistrust previously only reserved for estate agents and second-hand car salespeople (latterly, thanks to the likes of Fred Shred and then HSBC tax-avoidance scandal bank managers are now included in this elite group), there are still the scam merchants out there.

Recruitment is a great breeding ground for scams – when people need a job, they will drop their guard if they smell the chance of employment. And with job hunters' résumés/CV's sitting openly on job boards, it makes life that much easier for both the less than forthright recruitment consultant and scammer alike to gain information about you.

Scams can be straightforward minor transgressions, such as real recruitment consultants fishing (or *'phishing'* as it is usually called) to fill their database quota of potential recruits in various industries in order to get their managers to get off their backs. They will ask if you are interested in the position they have just told you about, lead you on about how great and well-suited you are to the job, say they are forwarding your CV . . . . . and then you'll never hear from them again.

Or they can be genuine fraudsters, asking you for money in order to gain you an interview. And thanks to the job boards that any Joe Soap can advertise a fake job on, scams of this nature are unfortunately increasing.

And while the job boards *"take any illegal activity seriously"*, well, we all know from watching consumer programmes on TV that all the internet giants, the social media websites, the auction websites, the budget airlines, the huge corporations you can't get through to speak to a human at, they all *"take everything seriously"*.

But the HR Cynics Society, of which I am chief executive officer (Ok, self-appointed, and with no HR intervention), will ask how you can possibly tell it's a database fishing trip or a scam.

Well, there are those little signs, the most obvious one being they contact you about how well suited you are for the welding technician job when in fact you are a specialist fish-farmer. So, unless *'my client'* (as they are wont to say) requires someone who can weld salmon, it's not you!

The *'I have a client who'* is usually a tell-tale sign that their client is in fact the poor HR sap we discussed earlier who omitted the *'no agencies'* from the recruitment advertisement they placed in the Evening Herald and Tribune. Said poor HR sap doesn't yet know it, but he or she is going to be inundated with agencies who all have the best candidate (at 25% of final salary as a fee) for the job.

Also, the monotonous *'I have a client who'*, or the grammatically incorrect *'my client are'* introduction can then be followed by, as every single client of every single recruitment consultant in the UK is, *'a leader in the field'*.

Despite being a *'leader'*, who, as a leader, would probably want to shout to the world that things are so good they are recruiting, the recruitment consultant will be very vague about which company is doing the recruiting, how much the salary is and where they are located.

This is also indicative of them being one of several recruitment people who have been allowed pitch for the job.

Naturally enough, they don't want you, the candidate, to run off to the company directly and threaten their commission.

The other thing recruitment consultants will do to obfuscate what they are up to, is rewrite the advertisement or even the job description itself. This can be done to the extent that you really don't know how the job title relates to the job description at all.

This is the scattergun approach taken by less than forthright recruitment consultants in an effort to close the net on as many people as possible in the vague hope that if they throw enough candidates at the recruiting organisation, one might stick and then they'll receive their commission.

This means that you the candidate will have great difficulty in demonstrating to the recruiting organisation's manager that you can actually do the job.

Those of you in living in the UK that are old enough may remember Comet, the electrical retailer. You'd casually wander into one of their stores, and if you looked attentively at the kettles or toasters, you'd be wilfully ignored.

However, if you looked at a fancy TV system or large range, expensive, warranty commission-laden cooker, assistants would be all over you in a rash.

Well visiting a recruitment consultant at their place of work is pretty much the same thing. You're either a cash cow for them, or it's a total waste of time for you, the candidate. Because it's a waste of time. They have the extremely annoying habit of inviting you in for an interview claiming they never put anyone in front of a client without assessing them first themselves.

Fairly laudable by all accounts I hear you say.

Yes. But no. Not really.

First of all, you have to dress up to the nines, and if a man, waste a perfectly good white shirt, to impress someone who might possibly look like a badly-dress car salesman themselves. Someone who will have enormous trouble keeping their face out of their smartphone. You have to put in time, effort and probably cost, to attend. You may, as a freelancer, have lost a day's pay. However, what you are doing in actually investing in the recruitment consultant. They are certainly, in most cases, certainly not investing in you.

However, the more dubious aspect is they are getting you in to sign away your rights to obtaining the job by other means, because the paperwork will in effect ask you to commit to them acting solely on your behalf.

And the most serious ramification of this is that of the job not necessarily being the consultant's to offer you in the first place. If they have been fishing for companies that are recruiting and have you in for an *'initial'* interview for a job they have spied advertised locally in the media, they are going to soil your chances if they then send off your details to the recruiting company's HR person on your behalf.

Because, if said HR person has already received numerous direct applications for the job at £x remuneration, if offered a slew of candidates via the recruitment consultant at £x+25% remuneration plus commission, even the dopiest of HR people will see through this.

So really, by completing and signing the paperwork the recruitment consultant gives you (no doubt on a clipboard – hooray!), all they are doing is protecting their own interests in terms of a fat, healthy commission thus ensuring the recruitment consultancy owner can continue their high life on the golf course.

Now, on a more technical level, no doubt you've been asked to submit your CV in Microsoft Word format. Well, quite a natural request if you have a CV to submit. But have you ever wondered why it's always Word and not, for example, a .pdf (Portable Document Format)?

Well, it's all about the recruitment consultant protecting their intellectual property rights, so to speak, namely, you the candidate. They need to be able to digitally scrub off your contact details, otherwise the recruiter might be able to contact and contract with you directly, thus cutting the recruitment consultant out of the 25% commission they duly don't deserve. And being in Word, it's simple.

Remember. The job from *'my client'*, the one that's still *'leading in their field'*, will all be speculative on the part of the recruitment consultant, so they may in fact have no contract in place with them, so should you go directly to *'my client'*, there's actually nothing the recruitment consultant can do – unless you've signed the exclusivity contract.

But, there is another and rather less than ethical side to the editable CV.

The fact it is editable.

This means that the *'helpful'* recruitment consultant can actually edit your CV (unless they have asked you to do it yourself – if you do remember to save it as something that identifies it and doesn't confuse it with the one you use for other job applications) to more closely match the job description. This is the honest *'economy with the truth'* part of recruitment. And you are probably at it anyway without their help as you add in electrical engineering experience that you don't actually have, as do all job hunters, even without the services of a recruitment consultant.

But what it means is that the recruitment consultant is editing your CV in their words.

And if either their standard of English (their, there, they're) or technical knowledge of your sector are lacking (and both usually are, judging by some of the appalling wording in their recruitment advertisements), this implies mistakes are being made in presentation, or unnecessary bull is being added on your behalf, and helping towards soiling your credibility

And the employer won't think *'the consultant rewrote it'* if they think your CV is lacking and you don't get the job. The buck stops with you as the CV holder.

Also, more worryingly, by adding hip and current terms you don't yourself use, you could get asked something about your CV that you don't really know about because you didn't write it!

But the fun can extend further than this.

Picture the scene.

You've put yourself forward for a job you've noticed, by sending your lovely, bright and correct CV in Word to a recruitment consultant (let's just pass on the *'my client'* and *'leading'* rubbish and forget whether he *is* *'database fishing'*, or not). He's interested, because *'my client'* wants to fill the position as quickly as possible, and the consultant invites you down to his office. You've done the filling in forms bit as well as the signing of your life away bit.

All goes tickety-boo for a few days, the consultant keeps you up to speed with his lack of any progress, and by the end of the week you're starting to have misgivings about the *'quickly as possible'* nature of this vacancy.

Then, speaking between clenched cheeks, the consultant phones to tell you that the position was either filled the previous day, someone internally was promoted or you weren't really the type of person *'my client'* was looking for. The consultant swears blind he'll keep a look out for a suitable and similar position and bids you good day.

Then you see a job in the evening newspaper that appears to be right up your street, and you excitedly apply. Perfect job description match, directly to the departmental manager.

But the company replies to you that they've already seen your CV and have decided not to progress your application further. And why is this? Because the recruiter you spoke to the previous week had speculatively sent their amended version of your CV to that particular recruiter, and said recruiter doesn't want to pay 25% over the top for a position he's advertising directly himself.

Because you've signed that blasted piece of paper, and the recruitment consultant will have told them so.

And so on.

You will be on the recruitment consultant's flavour of the month database. He (or she) will even send your CV out in response *to 'Mass-murderer required by local branch of the Triads'*, and despite your qualification as a computer programmer, he or she may even send it in response to the local care home looking for a plumber, or the local butcher looking for a meat packer, despite the fact you are clearly a mechanical engineer.

Now. What you also have to factor into all that has been mentioned above is that you may get put forward for a job you are neither interested in nor actually qualified for.

By and large, recruitment consultants don't care.

This is because everything is always so up in the air, with nothing contractual about anything, apart from the job contract when you do actually succeed in obtaining a position.

And they have a commission to chase.

In fact, there can be times where you are attending a job interview and you don't in fact know what it is you are being interviewed for.

Or for a job where no one seems to be listening to what you have to say regarding your skill set.

And so it goes. On and on.

Until said recruitment consultant drops you like you have a contagious disease. Simply because they called you with a job they assumed you'd be interested in but you decided that it wasn't. Irrespective of whether your skills set matched or not. Or, knowing you don't drive, it was in a pretty inaccessible part of the country that you couldn't actually get to unless you were happy with a 5am start with a three-hour commute everyday involving two buses, two trains and a taxi.

So, you have been dropped. From way up high. Despite the on-knees promise the recruitment consultant made to you to keep in touch, that their door is always open, that they are but a phone call away and that they'd love you to drop in for coffee and a Michelin Star restaurant meal next time you're passing.

By and large, recruitment consultants are full of wind. And bilge. They will tell you how wonderful you are and how they would treasure working for someone with your wonderful set of skills. They say they will always aim to get you the highest salary (and subsequently the largest commission they can for themselves) possible.

But it's really all a load of b*llox. Horse dung. Fiction. Nonsense. Lies. Fabrication. All they are after is a fat commission, and if it buggers your life up, well, as they say on the American shoot-em-up movies, you're simply *'collateral damage'*.

Let's have a look at what the recruitment consultant might say should he deem to actually call with some feedback about why you didn't get the job.

'The business has decided not to hire for this role at this time'

I'm sorry. But companies don't go to all the trouble of putting out job specifications, getting hold of recruitment consultants (even if they don't do that it voluntarily themselves) and interviewing people.

What it means is that the company decided that using the recruitment consultant and having to pay 25% was a waste money. Or at least that is what the managing director said to his HR person when he hit the roof upon hearing how much the recruitment consultant's take was.

Or that you as a highly-qualified mechanical engineer wasn't really the most suitably equipped for the clothing catalogue product description writer they were seeking.

'Sorry, but the position has already been filled'

Yep. The usual excuse the recruitment consultant has to give when the company says *'no'* to his commission-seeking advances.

Or that the company HR person already had someone in mind, but they used the services of a witless recruitment consultant or two to fill up the required numbers to be able to comply with the *'choose one from three'* tendering rule. They'd rather disappoint two strangers than two internal candidates. Pity the consultant didn't check that out before he suggested to you there was a job available.

'They felt you weren't actually a particularly good fit for the team and the role'

Yes. Despite being as good if not better than the person who got the job, the company doesn't want to have to add on the recruitment consultant's 25%, especially as the person who got the job came commission-free to the company by applying directly to their own recruitment advertisement.

The recruitment advertisement they forgot to add *'definitely no agencies'* to the foot of.

The final point where recruitment consultants can aggravate the candidate and their contacts is applying for candidate references where there is no job offer, or more immorally, where there is no chance of even an interview, let alone a job. Wasting the valuable time of your existing referees that could be used for a genuine job position.

There you have it.

The moral of the story is to watch out when using a recruitment consultant, particularly if you work in a niche sector.

Although, in all fairness, as I have mentioned, there are some very good recruitment consultants out there, far and few between thought they may be.

The good ones are the ones that have built up a great working relationship with their clients and have been retained by them for regular recruitment activities – yes, they can actually say *'my client'* without having to lie and cheat their way through a non-existent job for a client who is not theirs.

They're the ones who will take an interest in you and share your disappointment when you don't get the job they have put you forward for. And also fully explain the reasons rather than offer you vapid and churlish excuses.

They're the ones who won't worry one way or another if you can't manage to get in to see them before any interview they have arranged, as they work so well with their client, and are actually so knowledgeable themselves that they can read your CV themselves without the aid of a crutch. They will have been through it on the phone with you and asked intelligent questions.

They are the ones who do that magic of all tasks – they actually communicate with you.

These are the recruitment consultants you need to identify for yourself. The ones who can get you interviews.

If looking for a job, you will no doubt have registered on all the mind-numbingly dull, self-serving (for the owners), similar-looking job boards, all of which are bookmarked by every recruitment consultant in the land.

After all, the vast majority of consultants have no compunction about posting an identical job – real or imaginary - on all the job boards, just with slightly different wording. And the giveaway will always be the *'my client'*, *'leading'*, *'exciting position'* and *'rare, sought-after position'* nonsense.

Yes, finding a job without a recruitment consultant can often be hard work, despite the generic, catch-all job sites stating you should *'upload your CV and have recruiters rushing to you'*.

They don't and wont.

Unless there's something in it for them.

Another wonderful habit recruitment consultants have, and while this applies across the board, this irritation applies more to short-term, temporary contracts. And even more to short-term, temporary part-time contracts.

The job specification.

Yes, in order to kowtow to their *'leading client'* and take some steps to appear to provide at least some sort of return on investment for their fees for *'my client'* (i.e. attempt to justify their outlandish fees in relation to the actual amount of work they do), they will produce a job specification that would make even a parliamentary debate report look interesting.

Bearing in mind the job might be for six months for 20 hours a week, they will produce the almightiest guff that, were you sit down and diarise all that was being required via the job description, you'd need to be working for them full-time, 40 hours a week for at least two years to get through it all.

It's all part of the recruitment industry flannel that consistently proves worth outstrips value or cost by an unbelievably huge margin.

Remember the free headphone offer by a mobile phone company some time back – *'Free xxx headphones worth £89'* – yes, the recommended retail price might very well have been £89, but they were sold everywhere for £39, were available on popular online sites for around £24, and in reality, had an actual value of no more than about £9, if that.

Chapter 11

Now, stepping back to late 2014, Rachel Schraer, writing on co-research carried out by Reed Business Insight for the advertising agency TMP and Community Care Magazine found that that nearly 40% of social workers had a bad recruitment experience.

That is an awful lot of very important job-sector workers suffering and a huge and shameful dissatisfaction rate. As if it is not bad enough that social workers are amongst the most undervalued and underpaid, yet often proportionally the hardest-working people in society, many suffering excruciatingly uncial hours.

Imagine if 40% of taxis were involved in accidents? Or 40% of fast-food purchasers contracted food-poisoning?

There would be more than outrage and a national scandal.

What they had done was survey 2,100 social workers, but with a series of in-depth interviews, not just a single-question, tick-box survey.

Now bear in mind, if you will, that the list of ills was, frankly, frightening, taking into account the recruitment process is for such an important job function.

If the service provider was to be as bad at its care provision as it was at its HR and recruitment, this could be very worrying indeed.

However, the main bones of contention were:
1. *'Clever'* (!) jargon-filled recruitment advertisements full of self-congratulatory nonsense shouting how wonderful the organisation was and how wonderful it was to work there
2. Boring, repetitive corporate speak
3. Failing to give a job description and say what the role was actually all about and what the worker would subsequently be doing should they be employed
4. An application process lasting months with layers of corporate speak leaving the social worker unwaged for the period of recruitment
5. Losing documents
6. Interviewers unable to answer rather important and very pertinent questions
7. Huge fees taken by recruitment consultants that could otherwise have been paid to the hard-pressed and overworked social workers themselves

Almost without exception (an incredible 99%) of the social workers reported that having their application actually acknowledged in the first place would have been helpful (we've all been there – apart from an automatic acknowledgement from a job board, you rarely know whether your application has even been looked at or not, let alone rejected.

A very poor state of affairs given how simple it is to make a standard reply email template and just fill in emails address and name).

And again, an alarming rate of the workers (95%) wanted the application forms to be shorter and 98% wanted feedback on their application (this has become one of the recruitment industry's biggest bone of contention).

83% of the social workers said that a lengthy application form would put them off applying for a job (does any recruiter actually read a lengthy or any application form when a CV and follow-up interview can do such a remarkably efficient job?).

And 70% said they were less likely to apply for a job involving a personality test – well I've already covered the scenario of the *'do you like snooker'* on page 11 of the psychopathic test complementing the *'do you not like snooker'* on page two of the same test.

And in typical fashion, it was the social workers themselves who came up with far better suggestions than the HR industry could muster, namely:

• offering the chance for the potential worker to do a (very) short period unpaid work within the organisation as surely being a better way to show off their capabilities than just a regular, formal interview

• as part of the interview process providing the chance of doing a *'work day'* so the candidate can be assessed on their expertise and performance

Of course, the latter two points are altogether far too logical and sensible for the average clipboard-laden recruitment or HR person to comprehend or action, despite not requiring any way near the knowledge required for assembling a Hadron Collider.

The very sad thing to come out of this piece of research was that most social workers would not in fact promote their place of work to other potential social workers, with only a mere 13% saying they would.

That doesn't leave the social work customers in a very comfortable position.

It seems that poor management and poor support, including irregular supervision, limited continual professional development (CPD) opportunities and an organisational culture of blame were the culprits.

Now in fairness, this is not just HR and its operatives that are to blame, although, if HR is seen as lauded as being all that vital, it should share a very large part of the blame.

I just hope that the relevant authorities might get out of their OBE-chasing ivory towers and do something for these stressed and extremely societally-vital workers.

Now, call centres, for example, are notorious for ranting and raving about their continual professional development, but not actually doing anything about it.

'Your call is being recorded for training and monitoring purposes'.

Nope, that recording is purely for legal purposes and for covering their backs against the unscrupulous customer, of which, if we are being brutally honest, sadly there are many.

They base their staff advancement on either who has the biggest pair of lips to kiss the relevant laziest more-senior bottom, or on whose face fits the best.

Or who has the largest cleavage, and that's just the men.

Now, while heads of HR all over the world are known to suck up to their chief executives, immoral TUPE activities aside, as well as getting rid of staff aside, is there ever an upward, rather than a downward threat caused by these highly ineffectual and dysfunctional seniors?

The short answer is, yes.

Does anyone remember the rather infamous case of *'Neutron Mary'* as she was known, an otherwise beacon of light and excellent example of the HR industry at its worst?

Well, the chief executive officers of both biopharmaceutical corporation Pfizer and investment services corporation Schwab were dismissed by their respective boards as a result of one and the same head of HR, Neutron Mary, or Mary McLeod.

Yes, the same woman but two different industries.

She was well known for excessively using the Pfizer corporate helicopter for her own personal use, being both hard and abrupt with her staff and having a rather dictatorial control of relationships with the CEO at each of the two companies.

And successive HR seniors at the BBC (and there are an awful lot of them) have their own notoriety that includes outlandish remunerations (twice to three times than of the Prime Minister) and not being of this world, or at least, not being of the world of public service broadcasting despite happily taking the tax-payers' pounds.

Yet for all the fine HR people and their shudderingly-enormous salaries, while no doubt huffing and puffing equality, diversity and equality of opportunity at every available moment, still manage to get their 'stuff' so totally wrong.

The BBC, for example, are quite content with sending correspondents, with an established track record of demonising Israel, to the Middle East region, to the extent of bordering on anti-Semitism, rather than providing the independent, balanced and objective political commentary demanded by their charter.

And our licence fee.

So much so, that for all the fancy HR policies in place, their reportage is taken to task on an almost daily basis by the respected Honest Reporting, BBC Watch and UK Media Watch organisations, even on occasions attracting the attention of Israel Human Rights Watch.

So, something is intrinsically wrong in the state of BBC HR and begs the question are HR policies relating to equality, diversity and equality of opportunity really working there?

Plainly not.

What exactly are these HR people actually advocating amongst BBC staff then? Or are they even bothering to advocate or monitor anything at all? No, they are not, or so it would very much appear.

Aside from abusing company transport, being an abrupt and impersonal dictator, commanding a hugely disproportionate salary in relation to the work done or their net worth to the business or just being rather typically dysfunctional, there are several clear signs to choose from that can help an organisation decide whether it's about time to ditch that head of HR.

1. Your head of HR's closed-door policy has done a great job in gatekeeping your staff away from you to the extent that you never get to see or talk to any of them anymore. Recent recruits don't actually know who you are (and you don't know any of them either, despite you approving and providing their pay packets every month)
2. Your head of HR is doing a great job lining his/her own pocket
3. There is an impenetrable wall around the HR office despite other areas of the business collapsing and people being made redundant

4. Despite the impressive business card with more letters after their name than the average postman delivers in an average morning, your head of HR has a less than flattering nickname. (I once worked for a company where the head of HR was called 'Coco the Clown' – their crowning glory was being seen at peak evening viewing time on the BBC news, having a great conversational time and a good laugh with others behind the chief executive's back as he announced closures and redundancies on national TV)

5. Your head of HR doesn't really have a vision, despite speaking effluent jargon, boardroom bull and issuing edicts about *'taking the business forward'* on every conceivable occasions

6. Your head of HR doesn't really know what the business does and certainly doesn't know any of your customers, competitors, or their buying habits (I've already covered that point earlier)

7. Your head of HR still thinks email is altogether rather very modern technology and doesn't know what a Facebook, a Blog or a Twitter is, and has certainly never watched a YouTube and thinks cloud computing is the name of the company that provides *'those computer things to the office'*

8. If they are anyway technologically inclined, they don't have a photograph on their LinkedIn profile – ask why and you may have to call the police

9. Your head of HR has not one, not two, but three clipboards

10. Your head of HR's clipboards are fashion-coordinated

Now it's all very well blaming HR for all the business ills of the world, and yes, they well and truly are deserved of most of the blame thanks largely to how dysfunctional the HR industry as a whole has become. However, in the cause of bringing a little balance, the workplace can be quite happily dysfunctional its own without the assistance of, or cause by, HR.

It is natural for everyone to complain about their workplace. However, the demarcation between employees venting their spleens and there actually being something genuinely wrong can often blur.

Some of the problems below can be corrected if HR in the workplace was less dysfunctional.

However, other workplace problems - and it pains me to say this - area actually nothing whatsoever to do with HR. In fact, in some businesses where uniquely, HR actually plays a proper and forthright managed personnel function, it can be outside their control that the workers appear unhappy and are complaining. Even if HR is 100% spot-on, there are aspects of other management and direction that are totally outside their control. These include:

1. The boss chooses to remain anonymous, so no one actually knows who it is
2. The boss doesn't delegate anything to anyone
3. Nothing gets done without the boss passing or approving it. And if the boss is out, it never gets done. The only way is to go behind the boss's back
4. Too few team meetings are held, yet too many pointless meetings otherwise are

5. IT rules are ridiculously strict, so people miss out on third party remarks about the business or competition on the likes of the dreaded social media with its duck lips and purchased teeth

6. People throughout the business email each other instead of having face-to-face meetings. They also copy (CC) their customers, the local MP and even the rest of the world and its wife in on every email, even if the email is only asking the post-room when the final post of the day is

7. A director is hired because he or she is related to or friends with the boss. He or she is otherwise totally clueless about what the business does or who the business customers are. Or it's perhaps the clueless, top-of-the-range, mobile phone-addicted BMW-driving son

8. There is no coordination between departments' internal and external lunchtimes or breaks. This means sales can end up taking messages for finance

9. There is no real promotional structure and there are people in jobs that they are totally unsuited for and will never get fired or retired because, for example, they are the spouse of, or the boss's son

10. The boss goes mad over the most trivial of things, berating an employee in front of other employees

11. Billy in despatch is married to Joan in sales who is having an affair with John in marketing. Everyone knows this except Billy. And John's wife. Who just happens to be the boss's younger sister

12. People make sensible suggestions for improvement at the company that are never taken on board despite the fact they could save thousands of pounds or make the company more efficient

13. Many decisions are taken on a need-to-know basis, to the extent that new PC's arrive for everyone and the IT manager didn't know until they were delivered to his/her room.
14. No one takes responsibility for their lousy decisions
15. Everyone hides behind voicemail.

Chapter 12

One of the biggest problems with HR is that it is tarred with the same *'lack-of common sense'* brush. That is, if you take Health and Safety, everyone will tell you that before Health and Safety, people had only good old-fashioned common sense to rely on. They didn't need a procedure or a manual telling them not to test the microwave while taking a shower in the company shower room.

Unfortunately, while general health and safety (which falls, as I have mentioned, under the HR banner in many organisations) does involve a heavy element of common sense, HR does not. HR has, over the years, been largely made up. And as time passes, people are becoming increasingly scientific with how they apply these made-up HR principles, which is one of the problems.

People's employment, jobs and salaries are not scientific, so cannot really be pontificated upon by some college professor (who more than likely, despite his intelligence and clutch of degrees hanging on his wall, has never worked in the real, commercial world) in front of a roomful of prospective HR people.

There is no HR equivalent of an established safe procedure for lifting heavy weights. You can issue a sheet of paper showing someone bending at the knees rather than bending with their backs in order to pick up a heavy box.

You simply can't issue a sheet of paper with a little graphic printed thereon demonstrating someone 'HR'ing.

Now take this statement from an American chap called Harold Jarche that just about sums HR up.

'Work function silos are artefacts of a time when information was scarce and connections were few. That time is coming to pass.'

And a superb statement it is too. Even though I haven't the slightest clue what he is on about. And I am sure neither have many others. Work function silos? What on earth is that all about? Was he down on the farm? Or perhaps at the brewery making beer? Silos? Utter piffle.

This is all so typical of HR or even in fairness to him, boardroom bull, attempting to inject something that isn't, into what is otherwise nothing. Although I will admit the *'work function silo artefact'* I took to an antique valuation day one time was actually found to be worth . . . . absolutely nothing.

Now, talking about language, one area HR excels in is the use of buzzwords and phrases that are otherwise meaningless to all but those who have whiled away a day or two at an equally meaningless HR conference. In fairness, some of the rules relating to discrimination in language have been interpreted quite fully via HR, and deservedly so for those who can be discriminated against in the workplace. But let's face it, HR often have nothing better to do!

However, in typical HR-fashion, they have gone totally over the top in some respects, especially when it comes to *'man'* appearing in a word.

For example, a craftsman is now a craftsperson. And a chairman has become a chairperson, or in the case of those who are spectacularly wooden, a chair. The cleaning lady has now been demoted to cleaner and mankind is now humanity.

Heaven help us had HR been around when *'Brotherhood of Person'* won the Eurovision Song Contest for the UK, or Welsh rock outfit '*Man*' were at the height of their popularity back in the 1970's.

And if HR had got a hand on Percy Sledge's famous ballad when it was first released, I wonder would they have insisted it should have been changed *from 'When a Man loves a Woman'* to *'When a Person loves a Person'*. This would have to have been in order to reflect the double-whammy discrimination in the title relating on the one hand to men and women, and on the other to reflect lesbian and gay men (and not *'homosexuals'* HR will remind us) relationships.

Oh, and old man/woman/person, pensioner or senior citizen has to be referred to as an older person or elderly person.

I don't think the language used by many HR managers and practitioners helps much with the perception by people of its overall dysfunctionality.

For example, *'performance management'* conjures up complete unintelligible management-speak nonsense seen as an excuse to appraise (another bull term) people negatively. This is especially so when said appraisal is undertaken, as it nearly always is, by some poor, clueless, unqualified and disinterested line manager who submits said appraisal to HR.

Here, it will be filed, never to see the light again, most noticeably so when some vague promise that has been made to the appraised during said appraisal has no intention at all of being actioned by the useless HR department.

Some HR people, as if on auto-pilot, just have to use language that no one else in the business actually understands.

For example, in February 2015 a study by the Australian Human Resource Institute found that an astonishing 80 per cent of managers outside HR either did not *'understand or were unsure about what the human resources department does.'*

And in Canada, a global Mercer study found that an even-more astonishing 84 per cent of business executives admitted they had no more than a *'moderate'* understanding of the return provided by human resources to the organisation.

Now that, to me, is beyond frightening.

But it is true that HR has to use as much jargon and as many acronyms or HR whimsicals picked up from as many *'awesome'* American websites as it can, without hesitation or repetition, yet with as much deviation as possible, as they say on BBC Radio 4.

HR seem unable to say anything without referring to productivity, competitive advantage, revenue impact, innovation, talent management, talent mobility, talent acquisition, transformational management, pre-employment (ugh, *'pre'*) process, internal action learning, being more planful in approach, human capital analytics, risk management or impact on profit.

This is even though they probably know absolutely nothing about any of these things, given, as it is, that that tend to inhabit the outer worlds of some far-off galaxy. And I don't mean a chocolate bar or a Ford people-carrier.

It's like the humble financial advisor who has suddenly been gifted with the descriptive term *'wealth manager'*. This, at a time when people have less disposable income and subsequently less wealth available for managing than ever before. They have effectively talked themselves out of business, because some people will be embarrassed that they don't actually have any wealth to manage and would far prefer their existing finances to be simply advised upon!

However, to add insult to injury, there is no denying that all too often the vogue for HR is to refer to their people as an asset, a headcount, or even an employee number.

And now the utterly nonsensical term *'human capital'* is now being touted by some of the more fanciful (useless) recruitment consultancies (just say *'staff'* and stop being so ridiculous). But as Patrick McGoohan used to defend in that most complicated television series of the 60's, *'The Prisoner'*, – *'I am not a number. I am a free man'*.

But HR, more than any other department in an organisation, really has a duty of care to speak in simplified terms that everyone from bottom-up (and not top-down) can understand. From the cleaning person up to the financial director, everyone should be able to understand that their spade is just a spade and not *'a manual, up-and-over kinetic-energy transformational implement'*.

But this is what HR has sadly become since personnel management rebranded itself using the utterly ridiculous and derided *'Human Resource'* term. They brought it upon themselves and have no one else to blame – although being HR, I expect they have tried.

It's become a machine. And a not particularly well-oiled or modern one at that. A wind-up smart-phone in a battery-operated world.

But it's just a machine none the less. And it is not helped when, as a function, HR is outsourced. Because the external company will more than likely have been engaged because of the pure flannel it will have spouted at the tendering or interview stage. It will have really impressed the unknowledgeable and impressionable. Or director of HR as they are otherwise called.

HR has many annoying habits. As we as humans all have. But more so. And more of them. And unlike your partner biting their nails or picking their spots, you often can't tell HR to stop.

How many times have you been to an interview and watch the interviewer almost climax when you tell them you'd like to work at the company because you *'share their philosophy'* and have *'similar values'*?

You have? Oh you little liar you!

Do you really care that they ethically source the minor widgets they use that go to make up their major widgets?

No, of course you don't. You actually couldn't care less.

But really, what you want, need and like, is a fulfilling job. You really want to work at a job that you will really enjoy, that will pay you exceptionally well and will actually make a difference to the world. But then the HR director already has that job, and is pursuing it to the best of their inability on the golf course as you sit in your interview.

HR people love telling staff how wonderful the company is doing. Even though they have never met a customer and have absolutely no idea what the company actually does. They love gathering everyone together for a happy-clappy event before work one day and get everyone to punch their fist in the air with excitement.

It never crosses their mind that if the business is doing as well as they make out it is, the staff wouldn't object to, perhaps, a financial bonus.

This is a bit like the lonely shepherd.

Ordinarily, all they normally interact with is sheep. But in order to encourage the sheep to develop fine coats of wool and to cohabit with rams and produce little sheep, the shepherd has to ensure his sheep are a happy little flock. Or *'bunch'*, as the Americans infuriatingly refer to more than two of anything, be they animate or inanimate.

Too many sheep, and it gets a bit iffy and hard to control. Too few sheep, and the shepherd doesn't make any money.

So, like the humble shepherd, the HR person encourages a bit of cheering to set the mood for the people. He or she works on the basis that if all staff gather around together and shout for joy, some may actually believe it and work that little bit harder to ensure the next shout for joy is an absolute scream.

Chapter 13

I'll break off for a paragraph or three (how my weird mind works that I should think of this now) to recount a lovely scenario recounted from the film *'Algorithm'*. In it, Chris Panzera, who plays the character Will, remarked during his commentary that in the summer, the incidents of drowning increase.

Similarly, in the summer, the sales of ice cream increase.

So, the conclusion drawn is that ice cream is responsible for drownings.

And this, sadly, is the way HR thinks. The connection of two true yet otherwise unconnected facts to produce a false conclusion.

A bit frightening really. Well a lot frightening if truth be told.

Briefly mentioned already, team building is the great panacea that cures all the HR people's internal ills. They prefer team building to sex or food or both together, despite the fact it could get messy. They would scale a rocky mountain bare-footed to get to a team building how-to seminar.

And the words spouted at these seminars?

Why the following is the basic rundown of the editorial content of the sheet of paper on their clipboard. For those who don't understand the corporate terminology below, I have explained each term in layman's language:

Going forward – loose, meaningless and overused. Usually, 1st gear only. No more, but sometimes less. As in push-starting

To *'Action'* something – how about simply doing it? That's really so much easier

Touch base - about as meaningful as *'let's do lunch'*. Potentially a baseball reference to infer someone in HR actually does something active. Perhaps scoring an own goal

Circle back - to catch up later. Frequently used by the Sherriff in Cowboy films wanting to catch the immoral rancher diverting the Indians' drinking water

Blue-sky thinking – similar to *'thinking outside the box'*, they both translate as *'doing your job'*. Both meaningless. Unless your office is in the open air or you work in a box

Brainstorm – just like *'thought showers'*, similarly totally meaningless

Low hanging fruit - means nothing, as no one knows what tasks are actually being referred to. And not many mechanical engineering, governmental, accountant or lawyer premises, for example, have fruit trees in their offices. Or do they?

Get the ball rolling - simply means *'begin'*. Or in the case of Julio Iglesias the Spanish crooner, Begin the Begin

Drill down - not, as one might think, anything to do with heavy machinery. Unless an instruction from a manager to a man on the shop floor with a Black and Decker

End of play - curious strain of kiddy-talk in bureaucratese. Unless it's the end of *'Hamlet'*. That was a play

Deliverables – the postman always rings twice, especially with your e-bay parcel. Although some delivery firms are alleged to chuck it over your fence

Issues – no, they're problems. Stamp collectors often specialise in First-day Issues

Leverage – *'Give me a place to stand and I will move the world'*, said Archimedes. He didn't say he would leverage the deliverables matrix. The Arabs have been known to use oil as leverage against the West. It's the granddaddy of nouns converted to verbs and really just means the way Michael O'Leary extracts money from passengers

Stakeholders - wooden-spike-wielding vampire hunters

Competencies – nope, it's *'abilities'* or *'skills'*

Sunset – why call a spade a spade when you can cloy a euphemism? Ah sunset, that occurs *'at the end of the day'*

Core Competency – the opposite of core mediocrity. Great for those who are not too sure how much of an apple to eat

Buy-In – what some unqualified manager asks if you'll do after the fact because he didn't value you enough to discuss it with you in the first place. Poker players are often known to buy-in. But then dealing with HR is often a real gamble

Empower – the misspelling of a utility company

Corporate Values – sorry, but corporations don't have any values; the people who run them do. And they're usually all just about making money
Scalable – the venture capitalist's business nirvana craving. And the fishmonger delight
Solution - usually refers to a collection of technologies too abstract or complex to describe in a way that anyone would care about if they were explained in plain English. A solution is normally rather wet and contained in a bottle, glass or cup. Or a teapot. A solution is a solute in a solvent
Vertical – a painful expression referring to a specific area of expertise. Useful position to be able to maintain if you've just enjoyed an illicit liquid lunch
Robust - a cup of good coffee is robust. A software program is not. And calling the film *'Robustcop'* would have been silly
Giving 110% - to tell someone to give more than 100% is to also tell them that you failed maths in school. And Dettol kills 99.9% of all known germs, leaving the remaining 0.1% to kill you
Take it to the next level - in practice, it means nothing, mainly because nobody knows what the next level actually looks like and thus whether or not they've reached it. Bored MPs in Parliament usually have time to take Candy Crush Saga to the next level

As an aside, if you want to play a game at your place of work, photocopy this below that is simply the above terminology in tick-box form and tick the items off as they are referred to at your next HR gathering, that is, if you do have an *'allow the mushrooms out of the dark'* HR-led meeting in your place of work.

Going forward	'Action' something	Touch base
Circle back	Blue-sky thinking	Outside-the-box
Brainstorm	Low hanging fruit	Get the ball rolling
Drill down	End of play	Deliverables
Issues	Leverage	Stakeholders
Competencies	Sunset	Core Competency
Buy-In	Empower	Corporate Values
Scalable	Solution	Vertical
Robust	Giving 110%	Take it to the next level

In the HR world, team building is one in a long line of mushroom horticulture methods - keeping people in the dark and feeding them fertiliser of the pig-produced kind.

It inevitably always involves a hotel, coloured squares of paper, loud music, clipboards, break-out sessions and the complete waste of a day.

Now, the new fad that HR departments are now latching onto like leeches is *'lean'*. No, this is not sitting at your desk hanging over one side of your chair. It's a new - well not actually *'new-new'*- but relatively new in purely non-manufacturing environments.

I'll spend a little longer on this malaise, as it is actually interwoven with the origins of personnel management. It originated in manufacturing and is ostensibly a method of keeping the place running more efficiently and more cost effectively. And supposedly a little more clutter free.

Really rather sensible to be honest.

But in the HR world, it's a super-duper wheeze to keep the place tidy and stop workers from using their mobiles by ensuring they keep them off their desks (the mobile phones and not the workers – they get up on desks for all manner of reasons, some bordering on pornographic).

It also provides consultants (possibly related to one of the HR seniors, or from the firm the HR senior used to work in) with a humungous income at the expense of giving the workers a pay rise instead, and generally allows HR access to a whole new level of previously unused bull to explode out over the workforce's heads.

And it also involves clipboards, but on a really grand scale not previously rolled-out at a happy-clappy, jump-up-and-down-on-coloured-squares team building event.

Originally, it was car-maker Henry Ford who started *'process thinking'* about his manufacturing methods.

It involved lining up his production line components – he called it flow production – and it was the advent of the first real moving assembly line.

It also meant that rather than having a huge stock of parts all over the place, things were more ordered and he was able to turn his parts' inventory over every few days.

However, it was Taichii Ohno and Shigeo Shingo of the Toyota Motor Company who kicked off lean manufacturing big time. They began to integrate the Ford production method along with other techniques into something they called the *Toyota Production System* or *Just in Time*. It was they who, in typically Japanese fashion for doing things right first time, acknowledged that managed inventory played a central and very major part in overall efficiency and this production.

What Toyota had done was to apply Frederick Winslow Taylor's scientific management processes to the manufacturing process. Coupling them with a less harsh and ambivalent attitude to workers than Henry Ford had previously, they were able to turn out quality products that staff took pride in.

While the HR industry latterly took Frederick Winslow Taylor's idea and turned them into fully-fledged boardroom bull, Toyota and others were, by the 1980's, transforming themselves into World Class Manufacturers, something recognised by the internationally-awarded and highly-valued Shingo Prize (named, naturally enough, after that same Shigeo Shingo of Toyota Motor Company I mentioned a few paragraphs ago).

However, instead of becoming more productive, efficient and cost-effective and recognizing the value of workers, HR has taken lean principles into the office environment to simply get in the way of workers doing their jobs.

They seem to take the attitude that when things are quiet, you sweep the floors, clean your desks, empty the mousetraps and polish the office cat. And woe betides anyone who, when they are working, has a business reference manual on their desk where it can be accessed easily to answer a customer phone query as quickly and efficiently as possible.

Oh no!

Lean principles in HR terms means you maintain a clean desk by keeping your business reference manual tidily across the office in the filing cabinet, so that when a customer phones, you have to put them on hold for ten minutes longer than you would otherwise have done had your manual been conveniently accessible on the desk.

But that's HR for you. They specialise in fixing things that aren't even bent, let alone broken.

However, to once again inject a little defence on the side of HR – and remember, as I am sure you have all by now gathered, I abhor HR and all it stands for with a consummate passion, so the last thing I would ordinarily do is defend HR.

I have to be honest and say that business itself can tend to be rather chaotic at times.

It is, after all, the nature of the beast.

And if it was all so easy, everyone would be doing it for themselves (just like Aretha Franklin's sisters who were always doin' it for themselves. I don't know whether they actually achieved anything having done it for themselves. Perhaps they should have employed a consultant).

Competitiveness can see people in business being given time only to react to something rather than respond to it. For example, a market shift can be so sudden that even a Michelin 5-star HR department won't have time to respond when called upon by a panicking CEO.

And to be fair, effusive CEO's can sometimes make quite unreasonable demands of their HR departments. Particularly self-made CEO's who can be, by and large, somewhat useless themselves.

Not that I'm crying a river for HR. But all things are relative. Although, in all fairness, you can pick your friends but not your relatives.

But don't forget…….

HR people do love to hear their own bull spouted back at them, even if it has been previously copied and pasted by said HR people themselves. It gives them a sense of security and wellness (*'wellness'* another HR-friendly word – I always thought you had to fall down a wishing-well to feel in any way *'wellness'*) that there is an employee in the business who is as full of similar rubbish as they are. Therefore, you'll be seen as a fawning and possibly potential ally.

But just act like a London merchant banker, that is, be sincere to them, even if you don't mean it.

And keep smiling, as it makes them wonder what you are up to.

And don't forget to patronise them as if you were a 9-year-old with an eye on grandma's hand as she hovered over her purse.

Chapter 14

'What people don't know they will make up'.

This is a very important statement.

It is actually a vital statement that can ruin a business depending upon how it is interpreted by the business chiefs and their management. If businesses don't tell their workers what is going on, the workers will make it up. And if the workers make it up and then discuss it publicly outside the business, and that information is all wrong, it can destroy a business.

The simple definition of *'What people don't know they will make up'* is good old-fashioned rumour-mongering. Chinese whispers. Fiction.

Absolutely and definitely dangerous.

HR people are notoriously bad and ill-equipped at internal communications. They seem to have this self-destructive preference for keeping as much information to themselves as they can on their noe infamous *'need to know basis'*. Yes, certain information within the business will, by its nature, not be open to all and will - or even must - be kept confidential. Only a fool would expect the directorate of a business to open everything up to their workers.

Businesses aren't run that way.

However, HR people seem completely immune to keeping workers regularly informed about what is going on in the business. And they continually fail to realise that when the workers are kept ill-informed about things, mushroom style (kept in the dark and fed bull) they will make it up.

Another aspect handled by HR that has gone from bad to worse, when in really it should be going the other way and getting easier and better, is that of holiday arrangements.

Once upon a time, workers were given a holiday sheet to fill in which, after consulting the department holiday chart, they filled in and presented to, or discussed with, their manager. Said manager used to check the department diary or calendar and sign off said holiday.

Now everything is on-line, but unfortunately, also can be over-looked. It has been made so complex, in HR bull fashion, that the holiday process has become a nightmare for workers to arrange.

Instead of a one-step process of presenting a sheet of paper to a manager for signing, it now tramps its way digitally through the system, often either getting stuck in that system, pushed to one side, or just simply ignored.

The interview

Right, let's get a bit more practical, and look at the best outcome in the job-hunting process – **you get an interview**.

Now hopefully, it will be with your potential future line manager and not just the HR person alone – unless you are going for a junior HR job, then you have no option.

First thing you do on being greeted by whoever it is, is to extend a firm handshake (remember, you're not entering an arm-wrestling heat) and with a warm smile on your face say your *'hellos'*, to include a *'nice to meet you'* and a *'thank you for inviting me to interview'*.

If the interview is with an HR person only, unless it's a small organisation where they are familiar with the position in question, you'll get asked everything straight out of the HR text-book, except pertinent points about the actual job.

And if the HR person starts talking in *'hip'* and *'with-it'* language (*'And what exactly will **YOU** bring to the party?'*), try and resist any temptation to check whether your clenched fist fits *'exactly'* into their mouth.

To break the ice (unless you are interviewing in Lapland where this can be a dangerous occupation if the interview is held over a body of water), the first and second questions will generally be either the extremely pointless *'Tell me a little about yourself'* or the question you give every answer but the honest one to *'Why are you interested in the position?'*

You are presumably there, in your best bib and tucker having given up half a day, because you want a job and need the money.

Try to push all the practical thoughts that come rushing into your head to the back of your mind and bite your tongue.

Thoughts like, you moron - for gawd's sake, why are YOU here then? Is it for your health? Because you have nothing better to do? Are you taking two weeks off from the circus to fill in here and it's just I drew the short straw for this interview? Could you not even get a job in Woolworths? – despite it having closed down several years ago, something that shouldn't be too much of an obstacle for someone with your total lack of calibre.

Or have you simply fully-retired from the real world of work altogether and joined HR instead?.

Telling them a bit about yourself is not like you're asking them to transcribe your biography. If you can, put it in some form of context in relation to the job you are applying for (for example if it's a job in sales, you must mention that you've always been interested in selling) and compliment it with relevant personal facts.

They aren't interested in life's minutiae such as the brand of cereal your mother bought for you as a youngster; neither are they interested in you detailing the tours you were talked into on your past five holidays.

And don't mention that you regularly go to the pharmacy to take something for your kleptomania.

Regardless of whether you have filled in a long and laborious application form, or sent them a CV, sadly, the next question they will probably ask will be the old reliable and quite unimaginative *'run me through your career'* question.

While you may be sorely tempted to ask them *'Why, have you not read the application form/CV I spent ages writing?'* just give an outline of each position over the past few years with your key achievement's therein for each. In fairness to the HR person, they are perhaps checking that you and your CV actually matches.

Again, if you can relate it somehow to the job you are applying for *('I won an Oscar for the leading role in my last film, so I could possibly be a good choice for the lead in your film')*, this will help.

Any HR person, regardless of how thick they are, will always ask you what you know about the company, so make sure you have visited their website, read a few brochures, maybe checked up on who their customers or suppliers are and equated the position you are applying for with all this useful information you have garnered.

See if you can find out something about new products, awards or similar to show what a Smart-Alec you really are. But don't mention anything that might get a *'And how would you do this?'* question too early in the interview. The *'So how you would do it then?'* type of after-reply is a strong hitting response in the right context.

They will inevitably ask you about your current job, what you like about it, what you don't, what was your best achievement, why you left your old job and so on. The *'And what do you do?'* is certainly one of the most famous questions that was always attributed to the Duke of Edinburgh, rest his soul.

Be honest.

But if you indeed had a falling-out with your last position or you were let go because you were found taking advantage of the boss's daughter on the boardroom table, don't be that honest! The rule of thumb is to never knock any previous employment, unless you feel happy with declaring that you simply didn't like the previous job – however, if the previous job was in the same sector and position (for example, sales) as the one you are being interviewed for, take great care. You could talk yourself out of a prospective job.

Remember, the HR person interviewing you is, in this situation, a demi-god, whether you are religious or not.

This could adversely affect you and you could be perceived as being either unsuitable, hard to get along with or a quitter.

Best to just say you enjoyed all previous positions (unless it is known to the interviewer that this isn't the case) and that you are here today because it is a career progression (unless the salary is lower than the previous position you claimed to have enjoyed so much).

There will be all the usual suspect questions to follow, the depth of which will depend entirely upon the length of the interview:

Why you want to work at their company?
How you work under pressure?
Your greatest strength
Your greatest weakness
Your biggest success
Your biggest failure
Are you comfortable as part of a team?
Are you able to work on your own?
What if your manager is 20 years younger than you?
What motivates you?
What are your achievements?
Are you a clock-watcher?
Tell us about your hobbies
What are your salary expectations?

While many of the questions could very simply be, as mentioned, either answered by a re-read of your CV or asked by a complete moron, that's the way it goes with interviews. They have time to fill and need to demonstrate an air of importance that they have to maintain. Just bite your lip (in a *'speak-clearly'* kind of way) and don't answer like a politician, that is, mke sure you answer the questions you are asked.

And do speak English correctly, trying to avoid dropping either the "t" in the middle of words (it's Britain not Brih-ann) and the "g" at the end of gerunds (words ending in "ing"). And it's three thousand, not free fousand.

And don't forget the really pointless questions – the ones that are as pointless as they are dreaded by interviewees:

1. Where do you see yourself in five years? – at the supermarket, unless it's 7pm, then I'll possibly be eating dinner
2. Tell me about the time when you had to overcome an obstacle – someone left a large piece of wood in my driveway and I had to get out of the car to remove it before I could drive the car in
3. What would fellow workers say about you if they were here? – that it was my turn to get the tea in

Goodness only knows what these HR idiots make of the actual answers you give to these questions!

The final question will always be *'And do you have any questions for me?'*

Now, while you will be tempted to ask *'Can I have the job please'* (not an altogether unreasonable question - in fact, some say that in certain situations it can be a killer question that gives the interviewer no place to hide!

And if you're going for, say, a sales position, it can actually reflect well on you - providing you know in your heart of hearts that the interview went well) or *'Can I have your job please as you seem to be getting very well paid for doing bugger all'* (er, no, on second thoughts, better not ask that one), do have one or two in the bag to ask. It shows you are interested.

But whatever you do, don't be facile and ask irrelevant or Smart-Alec questions *('How many days' sick leave do I get?'* or *'Where do we go for our Christmas bash?'*). And don't ask questions for the sake of thinking asking questions is the right thing to do.

If you feel it is the case, tell the interviewer you have all the information you need and are happy not to ask questions for the sake of it.

If they run out of time interviewing you, that is their mismanagement fault and not yours (unless they told you to keep it brief and you decided to spend 40 minutes on your employment with MI5 at the expense of discussing your previous employment).

Should you not be offered the job, if they do offer feedback (that'll be the day), have no hesitation in taking it up with them if you justifiably feel the feedback reflected the fact that the HR person didn't have enough time to ask you all the questions they intended to.

But as I said, ensure it was their fault and not yours that you ran out of time.

There is one aspect of the interview where I do side with the interviewer, regardless of whether they are a consummate professional or an HR person.

And that is the candidate who is either late for the interview, or more unacceptably, doesn't turn up without even a cursory explanation.

Whether the interview is 100% genuine, a set-up, a waste of time or an insult to your intelligence, you, as the candidate, have the moral obligation to tell the interviewer (or the organisation's reception telephone if you haven't a direct number) if you are either running late or for some reason or other, can't manage to turn up.

It is simple courtesy and professionalism. And if you have a genuine reason, the interviewer will understand, rather than just leave them sitting there in the interview room wondering where you are. They are at liberty to waste their own time, but shouldn't have to waste time as a result of a thoughtless candidate.

Regardless of whether you are being interviewed for the job by an ennobled member of the House of Lords, or by 100 chimpanzees on typewriters trying to reproduce a line from a Shakespeare play, you have a duty to call in advance if you can't make your allotted interview time slot.

Back to the book

Hiding away in all the fear and loathing of HR people by the masses is a report by the Hays Group, who are, according to themselves, *'a global management consulting firm that works with leaders to transform strategy into reality'*. They also it seems, once again, according to themselves, *'develop talent, organise people to be more effective and motivate them to perform at their best'*. And they do all this from the goodness of their hearts. And give you a hefty bung for your time attending.

Seriously though, I can't say I've had a problem with the Hays Group over the years and have had a few temporary assignments from them.

Do please note that other global management consulting firms who work with leaders to transform strategy into reality are also available.

Anyway, the Hays Group issued a report in late 2014 (or it might have been early 2015 – let's not split hairs over a few months) that found relations between HR and line managers to be in a bad way.

It threw up (funnily enough, HR tends to make a lot of people throw up) that 41% of managers would rather consult the rather popular internet search engine (other less-popular search engines are available) for an answer to some personnel (or as they say in boardroom bull, a *'talent management'*) problem than they would consult the HR department.

Quelle surprise!

Although, to be fair, it **would** take a global management consulting firm that works with *'leaders'* to transform strategy into reality.

They also found that 40% of managers feel HR actively (never known HR to be active at anything except happy-clappy clipboardy things) blocks them (the managers) from making decisions and some 66% of managers believe HR guards data and information too closely.

By the same token, the survey found - and hang on to your seats here - HR professionals (professionals?) feel that the time they have to spend on management issues impinges on their key tasks (is that happy-clappy clipboardy time by any chance?) while over a third think HR spends too much time holding management and staff hands and not enough time on strategy.

Strategy?

HR wouldn't recognise a strategy if it strapped itself to their backs and dragged them over the Three Peaks Challenge!

And a whopping 94% of these dysfunctionaries (newly-invented word - HR does have some worth after all - quick, get me the telephone number for the Oxford English Dictionary) feel that more managers need to be empowered to make their own decisions, rather than considering talent management

This, translated into plain English, (*'matters relating to personnel'*), the sole remit (translated into plain English, *'function'*) of HR (translated into plain English, *'Human Remains'*).

As you can see for yourself, the overall picture painted of HR begs the question why it is here in the first place. And why there is a need for chartered organisation with such an overpaid directorate *'steering'* it, so doing with the equivalent of no license and never having driven previously in their lives.

It would be totally laughable were it not such a travesty, not only seriously affecting the lives of millions of workers, but causing such untold misery to everyone it ever comes into contact with!

Yep. That's HR for you!

Now I would imagine having read almost some 200 hundred or so odd (yes, some very odd) pages thus far (and thank you for that) you are probably wondering *'how is that bald, bearded, overweight chump qualified to write about HR?'*

Well, I do have to put my hands up and say *'I'm not!'* I'm merely a victim.

A very angry victim.

I'll give a little more insight in the next chapter.

Chapter 15

What I've written in this book is very much based on my personal experiences, my personal observances and those of my close friends, my acquaintances, frustrated real personnel people who hate the way the industry has gone, my experiences with DWP (the Department for Work and Pensions as both a contractor and one-time 'customer') and what I see and read in the media.

I am just committing to print what most sentient people have been saying about HR for years.

I have to confess that despite my membership of the World Society of HR Cynics, by and large, a healthy proportion of the interviews I have attended over the years have generally been quite good ones, even some of the contractual obligated time wasters where I was invited just to fill up the numbers.

Yes, there have been a number of them where it has been the relevant line manager accompanied by a furiously nodding and note-taking HR person, sitting there blatantly clueless about what was actually going on.

But by and large, interviews have, been OK.

I did, however, attend an interview in the not-too-distant past for a north London housing association that really annoyed me (the interview annoyed me more than the Housing Association).

It was meant to be held with the director of communications, a strategy manager, a lay member of the housing committee management and their HR consultant. Four people, I had been forewarned, would be sitting at the top table in the format presumably of speak no evil, see no evil, hear no evil and Evel Knievel.

Having travelled down from Leeds to London especially for the meeting, I ended up being interviewed by the HR woman alone, and a rather clueless, self-important, continually smart-phone checking woman. And she wasn't full-time with the business either, just a rather subjective contractor brought it for her *'expertise'*. I can only conclude form the interview that with her expertise she thought a housing association was an organisation that provides small green, plastic houses to Monopoly.

No apologies or explanations were given as to where the other members of the panel might be. I got the impression that she was going through the motions for purely cosmetic reasons, and that she had a crony lined up in the wings once the fakery of the interview process was completed. Or perhaps she had purposefully arranged my interview for 12 midday having arranged for the speak no evil, see no evil, hear no evil and Evel Knievel interview panel to arrive at 3pm.

I felt it was both immoral and unfair that the hiring process was being left to this one, subjective and somewhat clueless mobile phone-addict alone (I counted that she *'consulted'* her mobile phone seven times during the *'interview'*, on one occasion with a *'sorry I must take this call'*.

Indeed, a true recruitment professional.

Plus, the fact it had cost me a train fare, tube fares and lunch I wouldn't have otherwise bought, not much change from £90 for the day.

Sadly, I didn't say anything, which I should have done at the time. If only to appease my own annoyance with the highly unprofessional process.

On the other hand, some interviews have actually been somewhat enjoyable and extremely relevant.

I remember the interview process by a motor manufacturer that was appointing launch consultants throughout the country for their new car.

The first interview consisted of a visit to a recruitment consultant specialising in the motor trade who asked short, extremely relevant questions relating to the ability to cover a range marketing communications skills and being able to stand up in front of an audience.

In fact, he was thoroughly professional and knew exactly what he was talking about.

The second interview for the position was a rather practical one with members of the agency who were helping the manufacturer launch the car. No wandering at length through my CV asking puerile questions that the CV itself would have answered anyway.

They simply wanted to assess whether I (and the other 26 they wished to hire) could confidently present to motor dealers and whether we had the across-the-board marketing skills (and experience) needed that we could utilise to help dealers, especially the smaller ones who might not have their own marketing agency. And also to judge whether we could stand up in front of an audience and spout enthusiastically and knowledgeably about the product (after an intense three-week training course that would be held for successful candidates).

I was engaged to do the job and later went on to work for the manufacturer for 6½ years, again, thanks to an excellently-run interview with only the direct line managers at the company who knew and were directly involved with my work on the car launch for the five months previously.

If only all recruitment could generally be as sensible, logical, relevant and as professional as that was!

Another one that stood out like a sore thumb was a short 8-week interim position for a local council. Recognising that it was only for eight weeks, the head of communications at the council hired me by CV without even requiring a time-wasting interview.

Admittedly, first contact was through a small but very pro-active recruitment consultancy the council had a very good solo working relationship with.

But ever so logical and sensible. Having a long, drawn-out session for an eight-week contract really would have been ridiculous.

Like many, I've been on several complete-waste-of-time-and-they-bl**dy-well-knew-it-before-they-bl**dy-well-asked-me-to-attend-that-I-wouldn't-get-the-job interviews. I don't so much mind when the interview is local, and at worst, it's just time, wearing a white shirt that then has to be washed and ironed and maybe the odd car parking charge that is wasted. But when it involves a trip from Leeds or Manchester to London on behalf of a recruitment agency that is using me as a pawn with its *'my client'* nonsense, my blood does boil.

Two particular other examples remain in mind as typical of the complete thoughtlessness and ineptitude often exhibited by the recruitment industry.
A good few years ago I had a call from a Cheshire recruitment consultancy. They had matched my CV as being extremely suitable for a senior NHS post (yet another a *'my client'* of theirs) in Greater Manchester. They felt I really was a close fit for the job. However, there were two slight problems that surfaced.

The first thing was, it was a last-minute interview – I was alerted at 3.40pm on the Thursday afternoon for an 11.30 am interview on the Friday, less than 18 hours away when taking the travel into account. The agency had allegedly only been told late that morning.

The second slight obstacle was, it was in the centre of London. Cheapest day-return at that stage was an astounding £245 at the time. And I would receive no travel expenses. The saving grace was that the interview was across the road from King's Cross where the train terminated.

Luckily, I had a First Class travel voucher, earned from an unfortunate 3½-hour sit on a train outside Wakefield between 10pm and 2am a few weeks previously while the rail authorities scraped a very unfortunate and upsetting suicide jumper from the rails.

However, at the interview, I found out that I was one of the three candidates each of the eight NHS-preferred recruitment agencies (yes eight agencies – that's 24 external people, plus goodness knows how many internal candidates) had been asked to supply.

Now why on earth there had to be eight agencies is beyond me. By the nature of the job on offer, most of the candidates would probably have been registered with most of the eight agencies anyway.

Which means that in order to fill the quota, as the best-suited, cross-registered candidate-pool was exhausted; the agencies would run out of suitably-matched people and would have to resort to rent-a-crowd tactics.

To me, this defeated the whole purpose of the NHS having so many agencies on their roster in the first place.

The fact an internal candidate had been already-chosen was so obvious. Two of my three interviewers couldn't make it more clear that they were totally bored, indifferent and completely disinterested in the proceedings. It was a real *'contractual obligation'* interview, with me making up the numbers so as they did not fall foul of their rules.

Not a worry or bother about my expense to get there. And taking a full day out, not an offer of the £1,110 – and much more - they allow their own raft of non-medical consultants to suck out of the system for a day's *'work'*.

But what really needled me was the by-now infamous *'my client'* approach taken by the agency, the fact I had dropped everything (including a day's pay from the contract I was on at the time!) and that I had otherwise wasted a £245 First Class rail ticket to attend an interview for a position that had already gone to an internal candidate.

It is no wonder the administrative, non-medical side of the NHS is so derided while the likes of the wonderful ambulance medics, nurses and doctors at the sharp end suffer.

I did challenge the agency about the lack of information to help me make an informed decision in the first place whether I should attend the interview, but I could almost hear the *'so what, that's life'* shrugging of the shoulders at the other end of the phone.

Had I been on benefits at the time, my hopes would have been falsely raised, and I would have wasted either £245 of my own money or that of a DWP-provided rail ticket of similar value paid for by the tax-payer.

But this practice continues. It's like a disease. As soon as a public sector job is posted, irrespective of whether the organisation has posted in directly themselves on their own website, the recruitment agencies are over it like a rash, posting it everywhere as if it is theirs. And more so with part-time positions where Government departments, the NHS, councils, quangos or whatever post a job – there is virtually an agency infestation of *'my-client-ism'*.

It is truly horrific and shouldn't be allowed.

The second of the two interviews that particularly got up my proboscis was for a London-based rail group connected with HS2, the High Speed Rail project. At the time, I was appearing in a charity pantomime (as an Ugly Sister if you must know) that ran over five days.

The interview was late morning on one of the 'rest days' (only one evening performance as opposed to a matinee and evening), so I chose to drive so as to get straight back for the 8pm performance that night (nearly made it on time – arrived at 8:05pm and broke the world record for having makeup applied and getting into a huge pantomime dress).

The interview went well and I felt the interviewers were interested in my responses to their questioning. However, the following day I had a phone call telling me that they were very sorry but the position had gone to an internal member of staff.

Why couldn't they just have been honest and saved me the drive, expense and stress of trying to return home in a timely manner so as not to let the charity side down?

Or even as a rail authority, at least provided a free rail ticket?

Now what the recruitment agency didn't know was that I had an insider at HS2, a former colleague from DWP who had joined them whom I contacted. He told me that yes, it had been, what Private Eye magazine describe as yet another *'phil space'* exercise, where I was the unsuspecting person sent down to be the external patsy candidate! And not only that, there were several recruitment agencies (yes, in fairness, if that's the word) who were *'preferred suppliers'* all claiming HS2 to be *'my client'*.

I was less than pleased (I believe it's called fuming), especially as the traffic back to Leeds had been so horrific
Now I do know about all the tendering crap that goes on. Public sector organisations have to be seen as being fair by having at least some external people to choose from when it comes to recruitment.

But one only has to read the hallowed pages of the satirical magazine Private Eye to see that jobs-for-the-boys cronyism is alive and well and very much supported by many in senior public-life circles. I'm even convinced that the very expensive one-eighth page advertisements paid for by the very expensive recruitment con-sultants (sic) in what is left of the Sunday Times recruitment section are a total sham.

Virtually all the high-profile six-figure remunerated posts in there are already signed, sealed and delivered long before the newspaper hits the news-stand.

But that doesn't deter the high-flying, quaintly-named recruitment consultants, *'talent-acquisition'* managers and head-hunters from turning over a quick buck.

Because it's the dishonest and completely translucent nature of recruitment in the UK (and probably everywhere else for that matter) that gets me. All the fancy systems in place, talking all the talk and doing absolutely nothing.

Great at broken promises though!

Chapter 16

So, can HR be fixed rather than everyone continually hoping that it disappears? And do remember, as the old saying goes, a million Frenchmen can't be wrong – that is, unless they are wrong, or Italians in disguise, not that I'm pointing the finger at them for sheltering a future Iranian despot when no one else would touch him.

Many people have written at length on the subject of fixing HR. And I suppose, granting them the benefit of doubt, because someone has to do it, might perhaps be a more constructive comment than getting rid of the lot of them.

Companies, if they must have an HR honcho, really need to do their utmost to find the right person for the job. You need someone who is experienced rather than diploma-heavy and who has been out in the real world and actually achieved something.

The big problem to overcome is that with HR rotting away for the past few decades, there is much dead wood that thinks HR is a great profession for filling in the gap between pay days.

The last thing needed is a cheap fix. Someone who can fill the gap or is a pal of the chief executive.

Get someone good in there in the first place. Someone you'll be able to hold accountable for their actions. Someone who is not all wind and urine and has actually accomplished something relevant in people management. And make sure it someone who either hasn't got a bl**dy clipboard or who has, at the very least, an allergy to clipboards.

Something else to watch is that like business itself, the HR division (heaven help us all) has a clear direction to set out in and an equally, if not even clearer specification as to what it is they have to actually do. Don't let them get entrenched into HR bull mode – nip that in the bud.

And finally. Try and dispense with what has probably caused the downfall of HR in the first place. The distractions. The weeks spent organising the expensive and time-wasting happy-clappy bonding sessions that nobody wants. Free lunch in a hotel or not.

The things like quality standards and awards, the special projects that involve shuffling copious amounts of paper from one side of the desk to the other. Salary duties. Silly surveys. In fact, any of the nonsense that is usually the manure for the HR wastelands.

Ensure that you have HR honed to the state where if an employee asks for a private meeting with your HR person, they are not greeted with '*OK Yar. But it will have to wait until the back-end of next week as I have planning, implementation, training, teaching, chimpanzee-tea-party, bum-scratching and farting meetings all this week and for most of next week.*'

As I have already said. Nip it in the bud before the bull begins to make the HR fungus grow to the extent that if it is removed it just grows back again.

Story time. Another from the wacky world of HR. This time, Morrison's supermarket.

A friend of mine told me this one. Their relative was manager of the bakery department in one of the Morrison's supermarkets (other supermarkets are available, but I have to confess I do like my local one – staff are lovely and prices are great.

When I lived for a while in Guiseley near Leeds, Sir Ken Morrison himself used to sometimes serve behind the deli counter).

Anyway, back to the story.

This person had been working there for five years. Along came HR with one of those operations that not only do all workers know and love, but an operation that endears workers to HR even more.

The *'reapply for your own job'* scenario. One of the most despicable actions of any HR department. Or more so any organisation that gets its HR department to put staff through the stupid process for that matter.

Plainly lacking the nous to recognise that if they have two bakers working efficiently and effectively in their baking department, they don't need to ask the two of them to waste their time and reapply for their own jobs.

As a result of being too busy to fill in the form in time, despite her five years in the position, she was overlooked for the position she had held for five years. The position she had given her heart and soul to. The position she had run efficiently and effectively for five years.

And Morrison's lost an extremely effective and efficient – and more importantly - experienced bakery manageress. Nothing other than disgraceful. Well, absolutely farcical in fact.

I came across this particular form of HR nonsense way back in the early nineties when I worked for a Government-funded training organisation in Rotherham. It had been set up with staff seconded predominantly from the various local Employment Department (now DWP) divisions in South Yorkshire.

I presume the staff (apart from those brought in from the outside like the chief executive and myself) had applied for those positions within the organisations that they were both interested and qualified for.

Or at least the juniors were. I wasn't convinced that all of the seniors were 100% suited to their positions – they were simply senior civil servants who had been drafted in temporarily into equivalent directorate positions their own seniors in turn had felt were appropriate for them.

And some were good at it. For example, the financial lady plainly had fully-transferrable skills and ran the accounts department extremely efficiently.

The personnel man was also pretty good. It was one of the few times that I was given a full induction process to get to know what the various organisational departments were and what the people who ran them did in an organisation I was working for. And the seniors were all rather good at deciphering the government gobbled-gook that their then Department of Employment bosses threw at them for funding purposes.

After a few months, when things settled down, push came to shove in respect of those who wished to transfer across from the Employment Department and take up full-time positions.

Yet I was dumfounded to witness that the more junior members of staff had to then apply for their own jobs. Which seemed to me to be rather pointless. And the pointlessness was proven when my own assistant, a marketing and communications specialist, ended up in a non-marketing client services role, while my new assistant, an otherwise great and efficient young girl, transferred from client services to work for me with absolutely no prior marketing or communications experience.

A classic case of something that wasn't even remotely broken being fixed. An utterly pointless waste of time and effort as people who were fully-capable of doing the job they had been in for several months having to waste time attending internal interviews for their own jobs. And a process the chief executive should have put the stops on before it gathered the farcical momentum it ended up so doing. Reprehensible.

And as a result of this farcical change around of senior management, I myself sadly ended up with a *'director'* who was, to put it mildly, clueless. In fact, although I seldom boast, he should have been working for me, not the other way around. There was definite cronyism at work.

Now it's all very well continually knocking HR, and let's face it, the way it currently works, I am of the opinion it is well and truly deserved.

However, organisations themselves must bear some of the blame for recruitment ills. It's not all at the hands of the dysfunctional HR people, although they do have the power to influence. And where they work well in an organisation, they should be utilised.

It is only fair to mention again that some organisations have only themselves to blame, because where they actually have good HR people to hand, they don't allow them to do their job. I have seen this myself concerning the organisation I worked for that undertook the most dishonest and translucent of TUPE process. The HR rotten apple was at the top while the two subordinates were really very good but were never allowed to just get on with things and pass on their excellent knowledge and people-management skills.

In fact the Health and Safety manager proved there is life after common sense and he was only superb at his job.

Which can be a great shame where there are actually good HR people to hand.

Some of the common traps these organisations fall into include:

• failing to check if an existing employee might be suitable for a position. There could be the right person already employed by the company elsewhere
• not explaining the interview process properly, how long it might take and what it might involve
• having a set of criteria that might not necessarily allow otherwise perfectly suited candidates to apply
• using a recruitment process that suggests by so doing if you always do as you've always done, you'll only get what you always get. Potentially not the best
• continually looking for the 100% match – for example, the NHS have this terminal fascination with communication people having had experience of communicating for the NHS. Skills are transferable. An accountant is an accountant irrespective of the industry sector.
• taking a *'Phil Space'* (with apologies again to satirical magazine Private Eye) attitude to the job description by filling it with total waffle and utter piffle
• not involving the right people in the interview. Remember that interview for a housing association in London I told you about and that the entire process was conducted solely by some contracted recruiting consultant who plainly didn't understand what either the job or what I was all about
• utilising expensive, commission-chasing consultants whose only areas of expertise are bull, waffle and fees and who actually don't really know what or who they are recruiting

- halting the interviews having found the ideal candidate, despite there being three other shortlisted people to see
- offering feedback as to why a failed candidate was unsuccessful. Not having time to respond individually because there were 'too many applicants' is a very lame excuse.

Now employers themselves don't get off scot-free in all this. It's not just dysfunctional and dishonest HR practices, but sometimes dishonest and dysfunctional companies themselves. The ones that help sustain appalling HR.

These are the ones that lie, cheat and exaggerate to entice you to join them.

Firstly, some of the out and out lies they tell you.

'We will provide on-the-job-training' - (Amy will spend half an hour glossing over what you have to do followed by giving you some books to read . . . in your own time and at home please, but we won't pay you for the inconvenience)

Your work schedule can be flexible allowing you to balance your work-life, even working from home' - (when it suits us but we won't provide any equipment.

You'll have to use your own laptop and your own phone, neither of which we will pay for. And you'll have to call every hour from your home phone so we know you are at home)

There will be plenty of opportunity for advancement' - (well we think there is. If your face fits and you kiss the right backsides, you'll go far. Otherwise your main opportunity for advancement will be out the door)

There will be extensive training' - (that is, if we can be bothered and it doesn't cost too much and it doesn't give to too much to enable you to head off to a better-paid job)

'We can guarantee you some great interesting work that requires the expertise you will bring to the business' - (there's shed loads of stuff we have left until someone like you joined the business.

There's also a shed-load of boring administrative stuff that has gone ignored because John your manager thinks it's above him to do it)

'Your salary will double in no time' - (yes, in no time after you've been slogging away for us for at least a decade. We have a load of targets and performance indicators in place, so if you don't meet these, you haven't a cat's chance in hell of getting even a free pencil)

'You will have all the help and support you want' - (but not the help and support that you actually need. Sally from reception will help you stuff a few envelopes when the phone lines are quiet, and Don the post room man can sometimes help you shift a few boxes)

Secondly, some of the pure exaggerations you can be told when they need you as much as you need the job:

'We always only hire the best' - (indeed they do. The best for them and the best who are willing to work for them, not necessarily the best people from the job market)

'We have a 100% hands-off directorship style, employing you as the expert in what you do and leaving you to get on with it' - (it may be hands off, but it will continually be noses in. The monthly, farcical one-to-one will put paid to any hopes you have of a salary increase)

'A guaranteed work-life balance is built in for all employees' - (a few months in, we'll make you re-apply for your job and then re-employ you as a contractor, so if you want to take a day off at any time, you will be totally free to do so. Only we won't have to pay you for it)

'We have a fully open-door policy' - (but this doesn't mean you'll be able to tie any senior down for a chat if you have a problem. We just have open doors. Saves having to continually ask people to close them after they leave the room)

'There will be superb opportunities to travel' - (that is, for the directors. For golf. We have a second office 400 metres around the corner and down the road - a lovely walk in the summer)

'We see ourselves as an entrepreneurial start-up inside a large corporation' - (that is, we have to stay out of the limelight in case we fail and it reflects badly on the group. We're currently winging it)

'We are ahead of the pack in the technology we use' - (while it's all top flight PC stuff, it's been cobbled together from the main group's leftovers, so no two systems work together or are compatible. And Nigel the network man is almost bald from pulling his hair out trying to get the network more stable)

'For comfort, we have a totally casual dress code in place' - (don't wear anything too formal, because when our clueless HR person gives out to you about something she knows bugger-all about, you will soil your pants)

'Our open-plan office provides for a wonderful work environment' - (with virtually no privacy so that directors can spy on you and see that you are doing just your work and not faffing around o social media when you should be talking to clients.

And besides, the group wouldn't pay for any cubicles or office dividers when we started up)

What many interviewees – and probably even the interviewers, either through ignorance or on purpose - don't realise is that there are many questions that candidates really shouldn't be asked at interview. In fact, some are actually illegal (age-related and religion for example)

Here's a quick run-through:

Your age – Although employers can ask your age to see if you are old enough (for example, driving specific vehicles or operating heavy risk-associated machinery) they cannot ask you your age directly and neither are you obliged to place it on a CV or application form in advance. 'What year were you born?', 'When did you graduate?' and even the likes of 'Do you remember the Beatles?' are all questions that discriminators of those over the age of 50 like to utilise. Also, workplace insurance could be invalidated by a certain age range requirement by the organisation's insurers

How many children you have – it may seem like polite conversation with a prospective employer seeming to take an interest in you, but here you have a subliminal probe into how flexible a worker you are, evenings, weekend, early morning starts. This type of conversation should not take place in a formal interview

Religion – you don't have to say what religion you are and can politely say that you don't wish to discuss it but you can confirm that it won't get in the way. However, you do have a responsibility to think in advance of you have problems with say environmental or green issues, handling alcohol or certain foods. You are just as bad as the worst HR practitioner if you join a company with a work practice you disagree with and will subsequently expect that company to bow to your own personal life-style, especially if that company is not doing anything that would otherwise be illegal, untruthful, unethical or dishonest. And you demanding you light joss sticks on your desk once every three hours during the working day is a no-no

Your health – this is a difficult one, because someone, for example, with a back problem, should be sensible enough not to apply for a job involving lifting of weights. And there are situations where on-the-job insurance could be affected by the non-declaration of a health problem. There is not a problem with specific questions directly related to the job

Are there any debt problems – it is straightforwardly illegal to question you about your credit history. If the job involves the handling of money, then the employer has the right to ask your permission to undertake a credit check. For the majority of jobs, debt, or a lack of it, has nothing to do with your ability to do a job

Where you live – this could mean a job is being decided on location, which is discriminatory. If a relocation is required (for example a daily commute of 90 miles each way could be unreasonable for either party to sustain) it should be discussed. Although I knew of someone who commuted daily by car from Manchester to Scunthorpe for years, a distance of some 90 miles and both parties were perfectly happy

Is English your first language – this should be assessed from your CV and cannot be asked directly, as it could be interpreted as trying to indirectly find out your nationality. You can by all means be asked what other languages you speak, and if the position demands fluency in English, they should set you (and the other candidates) a practical (and the same) assessment test

When did you last use a *'naughty'* drug – yes, an employer has every right to ask if you are a drug addict, but cannot probe your past in this respect

Do you drink socially – another no-no. This one is not too likely to come up in the average interview, but you have to right to say no as it could discriminate against a recovered alcoholic

And as I start to approach the finishing-line of this book, I read an article in the Sunday Times newspaper written by Jonathan Leake where being overweight or obese is not a prohibited reason for discrimination (April 2016).

So, this didn't stop a Stuart Flint of Hallam University revealing that earlier in that month, in a study where 181 recruiters were given 181 identical CV's but with a photograph of the *'applicant'* showing them either *'fat'* or *'thin'*, almost without exception, the CV's with 'fat' people attached were universally rejected.

Again proving the total worthlessness of HR where they would have, in real life, rejected potentially brilliant people purely on the basis of their size.

Understandable if the recruiters were all either gym owners or weight-loss product manufacturers.

Chapter 17

In researching for this book I was amazed, or rather, should I say, dismayed by the number of HR commentators citing differences between Human Resource Management (HRM) and Personnel Management (PM).

I'm sorry. But this is a real wool-over-the-eyes exercise here.

They are very much one and the same thing. It's like Preston in Lancashire back in 2002. Up to 2001 it was a town. Then, in 2002, it was granted city status. Nothing really changed. It remained not exactly the most handsome of places. It didn't sprout a new national museum or art gallery. The people remained the same. The iconic and rather ugly bus station, despite being the largest of its kind in Europe, remained the same. The shops remained the same.

The transformation from Personnel to HR was similar.

HR remained personnel. Just stamping officialdom on the extra added bull that was being enforced on the unwilling workforces throughout the land – an on those of the personnel fraternity who are themselves hard-working and dedicated.

And plenty of it too.

I saw this when manning the desk at an HR exhibition in London when I was working for a government department in the mid-nineties.

This particular department was well-known for its exhibition freebie – the giveaway that ostensibly was meant to sit on the executive's desk to remind them of us and provide the relevant phone number and email to swiftly contact us should they have the requirement to do so.

The first difference between HR people and personnel people was that HR people came along for their freebie and then quickly disappeared on their quest to collect other freebies.

The personnel people, the ones with experience, the ones who actually cared for staff and knew what they were doing, would engage in conversation. They would present their business card. They would ask about any new legislation as relevant to the department I represented. And many pointed out to me, and were indeed proud, that they were good old-fashioned personnel people and not churned out by some University proud to have received £9,000 per annum for a bum on their lecture theatre seats.

They were people I would have been comfortable with in charge of my *'career path'*.

So, references to, and commentary about the differences between HRM and PM are in reality, total rubbish.

At least the commentators and *'experts'* acknowledge that HRM and PM do look after people management. So thankfully there is some common ground between the same ideal.

In comparing the same thing (ludicrous or what?), the experts immediately waffle into the nature of relations and the fact that there are two different perspectives to look at it all – Pluralist and Unitarist.

The experts go on to claim that good old-fashioned personnel were centralised while HRM works on an empowerment basis.

Oh really? Empowerment?

Empowerment to run fake TUPE processes. Empowerment to keep staff out of the loop? Empowerment to have some uninformed pencil-pusher straight out of university with no clue about what the workers in the business actually do on a day-to-day basis, or who its customers are? Empowerment to keep vital information from staff?

Then the experts go on to make us laugh out loud that HRM allows employees to play an important role as a part of a team to share management positions.

So, in essence, they think we, the workers are totally stupid?

Yes, and you thought it was only the politicians we vote for who treated us as if we are stupid. Being sincere because they have to in order to remain in office.

And then the experts have the temerity to claim that HRM is a *'win-win'* for employees by allowing them the freedom to select the style of working policies that can suit them and be of advantage to the organisation itself.

Yes, that is what these cloud-cuckoo clowns actually believe. One can only assume this is because they have told themselves it so often.

Then there's the subject of pay.

This, in case you didn't now, is the primary reason that people go to work. Here, the experts claim that pay policies, when handled in the good old days by personnel, were based simply on the skills and knowledge that workers needed for their jobs. They also say that in those days it was very much a division of labour and skills.

So presumably this explains why modern HR sees some of the internet giant directorate trousering huge salaries and not paying their fair share of corporate tax while using what little tax they do pay, possibly in deficit, to allow the government to top up their normal workers' below-average salaries on their greedy behalves? We saw plenty of examples of that during the COVID pandemic.

Yes, they claim that HRM encourages organisations to look beyond pay for functional responsibilities and to encourage a culture of increased job-performance and improvement linked to pay-related incentives.

So presumably, HRM is responsible, for example, for the banking and utility company fraternities' practice of rewarding failure and claiming that they have to pay bonuses to retain the best.

If that's the case, they need to shelve their HRM and go back to old-fashioned personnel where rewards are based on success.

Another area

Here are ten comparisons between HRM and personnel that the *'experts'* claim are the reasons modern-day HRM is so 'successful':

1.
Personnel Management (PM) is a traditional approach to managing people
Human Resource Management (HRM) is a modern way of managing people and their respective strengths
So, eggs used to be eggs, but not anymore. Now, thanks to HR, eggs are now eggs instead

2.
PM is about personnel administration, welfare of the employee and labour relations
HRM is about acquisition, development, motivation and maintenance of employees
So, bugger welfare and labour relations, let's get some HRM in

3.
PM sees its workers solely as an input to achieve a desired output

HRM sees people as a valuable and important input to achieve a desired output
So, lets organise a session on the last Friday of the month where adult employees can jump up and down on coloured squares in a bonding exercise

4.
PM was undertaken for the employees' satisfaction
HRM is undertaken for goal achievement
So, to hell with the employees, let's make the chief executive rich and ensure he only keeps his paid-for leased car for no more than 12 months before upgrading it

5.
PM organises jobs on the basis of the division of labour
HRM organises jobs on the basis of group/team work
So, don't allow the expert employees who know what they are doing run things

6.
PM didn't provide opportunities for training and development
HRM provides opportunities for training and development
Yes, only if your face fits in the eyes of partisan call-centre management

7.
Under PM, decisions are made by management in keeping with organisation rules
HRM allows for collective decision-making involving employee participation and authority
So, management used to dictate, but now employees have a say, which is largely ignored, and management dictate

8.
PM focuses on increased production and satisfied employees
HRM focuses on effectiveness, culture, productivity and employee participation
So, employees are no longer allowed to be satisfied at what they do

9.
PM is concerned with the personnel manager
HRM is concerned with all levels of managers
So, it's passing the buck to the ill-informed

10.
PM is a routine function
HRM is a strategic function
Bull time

And there you have it. Believe it if you will. Or must.

Chapter 18

So, instead of just knocking it, what exactly is the cure for this employment cancer called HR?

Well, I've already covered most of the cures as I have gone along. And yes, I reiterate there are some good, if not actually excellent employment agencies and HR people out there, although sadly for jobseekers (and the employers they fool) they are sadly in a firm minority.

I think the primary cure is for businesses and management to stop fooling themselves about HR and recognise how bad it is for business with its made-up nonsense, dishonesty and overarching and unwarranted power in the workplace.

It's time to normalise HR practices and bring them dragging and screaming into the real and practical business world. It needs to start looking after the interests of both the business and more importantly, its employees.

It calls itself *'Human'*, but there is in fact nothing human about it the way it treats workers. If heads have to roll, tough – they are quick enough to roll the heads of the workers for absolutely no apparent reason.

Whether or not the government of the day needs to step in is open for debate.

Certainly, employment agencies need to be regulated very harshly, as do the useless plethora of employment aggregating sites that have now – very much thanks to the shady practices of less than moral employment agencies and consultants – become a breeding ground for raising hopes and fooling people.

This, at the same time the owners of these aggregation sited make vast sums of money for doing absolutely nothing apart from hoodwink job seekers.

Perhaps recruitment consultants should be fined for posting fake jobs and phishing for candidates. Unless it is that they are genuinely working solely for *'my client'*, and can offer firm proof, they shouldn't be able to class an organisation as *'my client'*.

They (or the organisation) should state how many other agencies have the identical *'my client'* and like in financial services, they should declare both the rate of pay being offered for the job and the commission they are taking.

And organisations themselves should be transparent and declare how many agencies they have foolhardily put on the job. And Government agencies in particular, who are, after all using tax-payers' money, should be discouraged from engaging a multitude of agencies (or as they call it, *'preferred'* agencies) to search for candidates, especially as most candidates will be registered across a range of their *'preferred'* agency list anyway.

Organisations do share much of the responsibility, as they have to start being honest themselves. They too should be examined more closely for dishonest HR practices and farcical and often totally fictitious, lip-service TUPE processes they allow to happen on their premises.

And perhaps the CIPD has no need of a Charter. Has it outlived its usefulness? Does it really deserve, based on the current activity of British HR merchants and their business destruction performance, to have one?

I apologise if I seem very harsh in comment on those I have berated, but I have only written what the majority of workers say and feel but are unable to express it for fear of reprisal.

The entire kit and caboodle needs sorting out post haste before our children have to suffer like we all have over the past 25 years or so. The nettle needs grasping if companies are to progress within, which will have a huge impact on how the perform externally, that is, gain business.

It really is simply a case of treating people like people and cut out the archaic methods used thus far. Making employees feel they are an important part of the business, rather than keeping them on edge all the time is a must.
HR people have to be the workplaces nurses and not the workplace police.

And if that requires a complete overhaul, even starting again from first principles, then so be it.

Let me sign-off with an observance and perhaps another reason as to why I probably wrote this self-admittedly, quite acerbic tome, and I quote the entertaining Sunday Times columnist and film critic as well as occasional TV panel-show guest, Camilla Long who said:

'One of the joys of getting slightly older is that you just cannot put up with the bull any longer. Changing from someone who is happy to go along with others, to discovering I have opinions of my own, and being truly in touch with them, has been an amazing process.'

Yup. I agree. My only wish is that HR and all it stands for can RIP . . . . . as quickly as possible, before employment as we know it is totally broken beyond repair rather than it has been more recently, that is, fixed by HR when it was never actually broken in the first place.

Chapter 19

There is some very interesting research care of the World Employment Confederation (https://wecglobal.org). Admittedly, this has been somewhat skewed by the recent pandemic, as employment practices were forcibly changed, outside the control of everyone in the working world, to accommodate the ramifications of lockdowns, lacks of get-togethers (Downing Street apart!) and most dramatically, office working practices.

In fairness, we have never witnessed such a peace-time upheaval with respect to employment before in our lifetimes.

While at the time of updating this book, some organisations have been happy to continue working remotely, more so to dispense with the high cost of office space and rates, and now, energy prices. This is understandable, but the knock-on effect for city centres has been more than dramatic, with the catering and hospitality trade becoming ever-more reliant on business from leisure spenders rather than day-time office spenders.

It's all about being able to flexibly adapt to the current state of the nation. Something like a pandemic takes no prisoners, so it has been thrown at firms to adapt, and with some of them, that adaptation has produced many positives (along with the negatives).

It has been proven that taking the stress of travel, whether by car with traffic jams and expensive parking, or by public transport than can often not run like clockwork, office workers have discovered the joy of raising from their beds at 8.25 instead of 6.45 to get to work for 9am.

Yes, there is the disadvantage that workers don't meet and see fellow works as much, but knowing that, and aside from the start of day advantages already mentioned, leaving your desk at 5.30pm and being home in the kitchen to prepare dinner at 5.35pm has very distinct advantages in term of time spent either in the car or on public transport getting back home.

These are some of the mind-blowing statistics from around the world, with sincere thanks to the World Employment Confederation (the latest figures available at the time of publication were for 2020).

2020
Private employment services industry global market €465.8 billion (yes, you read that correctly!)

Agency revenues - €361.4 billion
Managed service provision - €37.8 billion
Direct recruitment activities - €59.4 billion
Recruitment process outsourcing - €5.1 billion
Career management market - €2.2 billion

There were some 190,000 private employment agencies operating in the 40 countries the Confederation received figures from, with 3.7 million staff.

Placements by private employment agencies – 58 million
Placements through direct recruitment – 3 million
Temporary worker placements – 55 million

30 countries in Europe
9 million placements
75,500 private employment agencies
373,600 staff
Agency revenues - €145.3 billion
Managed service provision - €41.7 billion
Direct recruitment activities - €17.6 billion
Recruitment process outsourcing - €1.5 billion

Canada, Mexico, USA
18.9 million placements
27,300 private employment agencies
460,300 staff
Agency revenues - €113.3 billion
Managed service provision - €72.2 billion
Direct recruitment activities - €15.8 billion
Recruitment process outsourcing - €2.3 billion

Argentina, Brazil, Chile, Colombia
0.9 million placements
5,500 private employment agencies
350,000 staff
Agency revenues - €2.6 billion
Managed service provision - €2.2 billion
Direct recruitment activities - €0.3 billion
Recruitment process outsourcing - €0.2 billion

Australia, China, India, Indonesia. Japan, New Zealand

28.2 million placements
67,100 private employment agencies
948,000 staff
Agency revenues - €95.3 billion
Managed service provision - €12.6 billion
Direct recruitment activities - €24.9 billion
Recruitment process outsourcing - €1.0 billion

Postscript

During the final fortnight finishing off the first edition of this book in 2016, proofreading yet again (and still finding mistakes – sorry if some still crept through) and putting the finishing touches to the cover, I was approached by one of the better national recruitment consultancies regarding a short-term contract position as Senior Communications Manager for an NHS Trust's (non-medical) patient transport service.

The consultant was as gob-smacked and frustrated as myself when the results of the CV reviews were returned and it was suggested by the patient transport people (presumably their HR people) that they were concerned at my *'lack of NHS experience'*.

As the consultant agreed, this was the same as saying a qualified high street butcher is not suited for working for Morrison's because they don't have supermarket experience, or telling a pub chain accountant they don't have enough hotel experience to book-keep for hotel chain.

It's called transferrable skills.

If you have a qualification in accountancy, then you can count the figures in any business. Similarly, with a qualification in marketing communications (as well as over 30 years' experience), you can Press and PR-ise in any business.

However, the nail in the stupidity coffin on the part of this patient transport service was the fact that I already had seven months' experience working for a ...... patient transport organisation, just a couple of years previously. And remember, this was only for a short-term contract, so why they were making such a mountain out of a molehill in the first place defies belief.

This is just more proof to support my argument as to how dysfunctional HR has become. It's not that I necessarily held particular or definite expectation that I would get the job, but given my experience, the consultant was almost rock-solidly sure I would at least be offered an interview.

And as I mentioned. I had previously obtained the Wrexham Council position purely from my CV and without an interview . . . . I went in with absolutely no prior experience of working for a Council. The very intelligent and switched-on manageress realised from my CV that I had the skills she was seeking for what was a quick 8-week fix.

And as I mentioned, it was a very successful and fulfilling one for both parties.

Case proven and closed.

However, what is perhaps laughable, but by no means funny, is that with all the fancy HR systems in place, while they overflow with fancy, twee statements such *as 'people matter', 'our strongest asset is our people', 'staff first'* and more, many companies, organisations and corporations continue to treat their staff with total and utter contempt as the directorate haul their eye-watering salaries to the bank and their perks back to their homes.

Today's employees seem to face incredible barriers to job security that simply did not exist ten to fifteen years ago. They say that a dog is for life, not just for Christmas. Employment, on the other hand, seems to be just for Christmas and no longer for life.

All the fancy human resources, one-to-ones, balanced scorecards, psychometric testing, behavioural characteristics and the rest of the HR nonsense will simply continue to pay lip service to hard-pressed staff members who deserve better than the contrived clipboard culture they currently receive.

So come on HR.

Get your collective acts together. You owe it to both your workers and potential workers alike.

www.ingramcontent.com/pod-product-compliance
Lightning Source LLC
Chambersburg PA
CBHW052346220526
45465CB00003BA/987